T0065544

My Encounter With Jesus At Heaven's Gates

- A Life-changing Near Death Experience

SANTOSH (SANDY) ACHARJEE

authorHOUSE®

AuthorHouse™
1663 Liberty Drive
Bloomington, IN 47403
www.authorhouse.com
Phone: 1 (800) 839-8640

Published by AuthorHouse   09/07/2016

ISBN: 978-1-5246-2810-9 (sc)
ISBN: 978-1-5246-2809-3 (e)

Library of Congress Control Number: 2016914663

Print information available on the last page.

NIV
Scripture quotations marked NIV are taken from the Holy Bible, New International Version®. NIV®. Copyright © 1973, 1978, 1984 by International Bible Society. Used by permission of Zondervan. All rights reserved. [Biblica]

NKJV
Scripture quotations marked NKJV are taken from the New King James Version. Copyright © 1982 by Thomas Nelson, Inc. Used by permission. All rights reserved.

KJV
Scripture quotations marked KJV are from the Holy Bible, King James Version (Authorized Version). First published in 1611. Quoted from the KJV Classic Reference Bible, Copyright © 1983 by The Zondervan Corporation.

Book Dedication Page

This book is dedicated to any person from any religion, any culture or any background who truly wants to know the Truth

Contents

Editor Lauraine Myers' Notes ix

Pastor Steve Harper's Notes xi

Editor Marilyn Neale's Notes xiii

Prologue for the New Edition xvii

Acknowledgements for the New Edition xxi

Acknowledgements for the First Book – A Miraculous True Story xxv

Introduction Of The First Book 1

Sudden Crisis In Life 5

Further Complications At ICU 9

Death Or Near Death Experience 16

Journey To An Unknown Destination 20

Magnificent Beauty Of Heaven 22

Face To Face With God In Heaven 24

Loving God & The Narrow Door 27

Return To Earth At Critical Care Unit 30

Readjustment After Return 32

Beginning Of A Miraculous Recovery 35

Recollection Of Events 41

Gangrenous Gall Bladder 44

Mini Surgery & Oxygen Therapy 47

Major Lung Surgery 50

Amazing Bounce Back To Life 55

Unexpected Apology From Dr. X 58

Conversation With God 60

Specific Instructions From God 63

Release From The Hospital 69

Return To Regular Activities 71

Inspiration 73

Author's Note 75

Readers' Testimonials about Code Blue 99 77

Confusion and Dilemma 85

Resolution 90

What is the Truth? 95

What Does God Look Like? 102

Love Your Family & Love Your Children 109

Where Can We Find God? 118

Religions and God 124

Believeth in Me! 131

Surrender Yourself Completely Unto Me in Your Daily Lives! 142

Meditation & Prayers 145

Walk With Me 150

Heaven & Hell 157

Follow Darkness or the Light? 161

Follow Jesus if you want to go through the Narrow Door 175

Take Care Of The Poor 188

Bible Credits 191

Editor Lauraine Myers' Notes

Ecclesiastes tell us that God has set eternity in the heart of every man (mankind) (Ecclesiastes 3:11). It is inherent for man to seek **something**, to satisfy the inherent deep need to answer the question relative to eternity; 'where will I go when I die?' We will not, inherently, rest until this has been satisfied. This is both a declaration of the human soul as well as our flawed human nature. This is the chasm between our seen world and an unseen final destination. Eternity is written on our hearts by the finger of God and thus we cannot utterly blot it out or ignore it. And so we, in our limited ways and resources, attempt to find the answers in the world that has been set before us.

God has chosen Santosh for this dramatic experience; a kind of experience that would violently shake him from a religious background and culture, where images of empty gods, culture and a way of life that was all around him, where he knew of nothing else - to profoundly state that all of it - **all of it** - didn't and doesn't matter.

This is a message of pursuit. Santosh speaks of the devastation of a father over a loss of a child demonstrating a fierce expression of love. What God has provided for us, the gift of salvation, through the death and resurrection of Jesus Christ, is a message of our Heavenly Father's fierce statement of love, pursuing hard after us.

Throughout this process, I have learned many things about Santosh. He has a peaceful, contentment about him that is practically tangible, especially when he speaks, without wavering, the love, compassion and mercy of God – a firsthand experience. I have often thought about Santosh's background; the saturation of Hinduism in his life and the depth of this saturation based on the historical thousands upon thousands of years of its existence is undeniably considerable. The manner in which he was dramatically converted, having been freed from a darkness, which is his message, is such a profound encouragement for those to break away from what is known and comfortable, that the promises of God are far better than our temporary state, however you might describe or define it. Jesus said,

> *"Truly I say to you, there is no one who has left house or wife or brothers or parents or children, for the sake of the Kingdom of God, who will not receive many times as much at this time and in the age to come, eternal life."* Luke 18:29-30 NASB

Follow Santosh's journey from beginning to end and you will become affected by the details of his tumultuous health sufferings to the dramatic exit of his life, suddenly catapulting him into the presence of the King of Kings to learn first-hand, the answer to the question, 'what is the Truth?', or rather, **Who** is the Truth? While Santosh conveys the gravity of our decision, it is told with love and understanding and through the eyes of a changed man from a culture I am completely unfamiliar with. God, in His grace and mercy, has allowed all those who remain alive, a glimpse of the answer to the inherent question relative to eternity; 'where will I go when I die?'

Follow this experience with him, as he states often that religion has no value or contribution to your eternal destiny that it is only and solely accomplished by the power of experience through the Holy Spirit that changes lives dramatically, *"Truly, truly, I say to you, unless one is born again, he cannot see the kingdom of God."* John 3:3 NASB

This is God's continued expression of His love for us, though Jesus, to prepare us for His soon return, instilling the message of our God longing for an intimate relationship, such that when we have our turn, as Santosh did, standing before Him at Heaven's Gate, we can hear God say, *"Enter in,* (calling us by name) *I know who you are."* (Ref. Matt 7:21-23 (paraphr.))

Lauraine Myers
Editor

Pastor Steve Harper's Notes

I met Santosh at his baptism on April 12, 2015. The congregation gasped as Santosh spoke with clarity and conviction about his near death experience. As Santosh's book describes, all the gates of heaven were closed to him and the flames of hell were his final destination had Jesus not given him a second chance. Santosh begged Jesus for mercy and surrendered his life to Him! When he told me the full details of his story, I immediately thought of the apostle Paul's words, "We must all appear before the judgment seat of Christ" (2 Corinthians 5:10) and Jesus' words,

> "'As surely as I live,' says the Lord, 'every knee will bend to me, and every tongue will declare allegiance to God.'" (Romans 14:10-11 NLT).

Santosh's experience with Jesus as well as heaven and hell, they all line up with the Scriptures. Even though he was raised a Hindu, he had no knowledge of the Scriptures at that time. The six things Jesus told Santosh to do upon his return to earth are Biblical and instructive for each of us who wants to make a difference with our lives and please God!

The transformation in Santosh's life and his devotion to Jesus authenticates his story to me. When I am with him, I feel like I'm with one of the apostles who walked with Jesus. His life isn't perfect, but he lives for a perfect Savior!

May you sense God's presence in your life as you read Santosh's account of the afterlife and may you surrender to Jesus and experience His transforming power!

Gratefully,
Steve Harper Associate Pastor, Grace Church, Middleburg Heights, Ohio

Editor Marilyn Neale's Notes

Sandy has asked me to write a few words as an introduction to this wonderful book. He also suggested that I pray to the Holy Spirit before doing so. That, of course, is a wonderful way to start anything we attempt to do in our lives. Actually, as I closed my eyes while sitting in front of the computer, I said to the Holy Spirit, "I think I will just be still and listen to You, instead of requesting assistance, guidance, or particular words." So that is what I'm doing at this very moment - listening. I feel that whatever is being typed is coming directly from our Divine Lord through the Holy Spirit.

If you have read Sandy's previous books, "Code Blue 99 – A Miraculous True Story!" and "The Light, The Truth, and The Way," you know, by reading the Editor's Notes, that I feel I was called by God to be involved in the editing and publishing of them. My husband, Ted, and I are dear friends of his, and circumstances were so that we both, actually, became involved. I have done the editing, and Ted has been there to give additional input on various topics and questions, along with encouragement.

Sandy's story of "death" and return to this life is an extraordinary one. For many years, as an adolescent and adult, I have been very interested in these types of stories. However, most of the books and films that contain "similar" experiences lack the huge message that is contained in these three books. In none of the books I have read or movies I have seen previously did I find the extensive and divine message that The Lord has given Sandy to share with the entire world. Most of them only briefly explain their "out-of-body" experience, going through the tunnel of light, meeting with loved ones, a few brief encounters with God, etc.

Sandy's experience, however, is so extremely different. Just the circumstances of his death (with multiple serious physical conditions that caused his death) and the healing that took place even before his return to this life were "miraculous." His conversations with the Lord were so personal, extensive and specific.

Heal me, O Lord, and I will be healed;
save me and I will be saved, for you are the one I praise
(Jeremiah 17:14)

Additionally, Sandy has included many passages in the book that were almost identical to that written in the Bible. This is a very important point to consider, since he had never been exposed to the Bible, having been raised a Hindu. This, again, is proof that he truly had a very special connection/encounter with The Lord after his "death."

You will know the truth,
and the truth will set you free.
(John 8:32)

Both Sandy and I have been adamant in feeling that this message from The Lord MUST reach everyone, particularly at this dire time in our lives. It is imperative that it be heard literally by everyone. Hence, we have tried to find the right avenues to spread His word. With God's help, we will.

Blessed is the man who trusts in the Lord,
whose confidence is in him.
(Jeremiah 17: 7)

When you read this book, please "study" it and its contents,
which are extremely important for our eternal salvation.
Only if we heed and follow the instructions of The Lord
will we be able to enter into His Kingdom..

The world and its desires pass away, but
the man who does the will of God lives forever.
(1 John 2:17)

But our citizenship is in heaven.
And we eagerly await a Savior from
there, the Lord Jesus Christ.
(Philippians 3:20)

Marilyn Neale
Editor

Prologue for the New Edition

The Lord has been telling me that the time is now appropriate for me to edit the two books that I wrote earlier. The first one was "Code Blue 99, - A Miraculous True Story!" and, the second one was "The Light, The Truth, and The Way." I can clearly see how God has used the two books for me to find the Truth and helped me grow substantially in my relationship with Him. Therefore, I think it is ideal to combine the two books into a new edition, with a new title. Let me explain my reasoning.

First of all, I never wrote a book in my life, nor did I have any intention to do so at any time. The Lord asked me to write the two books when I encountered Him unexpectedly in October 2006. I had no alternative but to write them just to comply with His Instructions. During the Encounter, the Lord had said to me that He will see me again next time. Truly speaking, I simply do not have the courage to face the Lord during my next time unless I complied with His Instructions. To not obey would be a fatal mistake on my part, and I would not dare to commit such a mistake. During my Encounter, the Lord appeared to me as a huge Giant, and I was absolutely powerless in front of Him.

However, it has been almost 10 years since I wrote the first book and about 8 years since I wrote the second book. To be totally frank with you, at the time I wrote both of these books, my knowledge of the Scriptures was very limited. I had never studied the Bible, nor had I read any other religious books, because I never felt the need to do so. Reading any such books was always at the lowest level of my priorities. I even considered it to be a complete waste of my valuable time.

Today, I know one thing - this unexpected Encounter with the Lord has changed me completely. The way I think now is totally opposed to the way I thought previously. After all these years, I could never erase from my memories all the things that I witnessed during the three-day Encounter with the Lord. All the things I witnessed there were all real. They were not dreams.

The Hell, with its frightening darkness and only visible light of burning lakes of fire, where I was destined to fall from the platform with no railings, located on an abyss was real. The magnificent beauty of the Kingdom of Heaven in front of me, with gorgeous walls and many superb mansions inside the compound, was real. The presence of numerous angels, including their abilities to fly and administer, was real. Witnessing the 12 marvelous Gates that were closed for me to enter into the Kingdom, was real. The Face-to-face Encounter with the, Lord was real. Heart-to-heart conversation with the Lord, was real. Witnessing the one and only Narrow Door that was open for me to enter, was real. Although the Narrow Door was open for me to enter, I would not dare to do so unless and until the Lord gave me permission. Nobody can dare to enter through that Narrow Door unless the Lord lets him/her in.

Yet, to this day, His Love, His Mercy, and His Grace to me are all real. Sending me back to the earth and giving me a second chance in this life are real. Healing me from my incurable health issues without any medications is real. How can I deny any of them? As long as I live and until He sees me again next time, I can never forget any of them.

However, I must admit to you that I was quite confused after my return from the Encounter with the Lord. Even though I wrote the two books as per His Instructions, I was continuously searching for the Truth. What are the meanings of all the things that I witnessed? How can I find their true answers? Where can I get them? I was desperately searching for their meanings as I was seeking the Truth. I needed to know what they meant.

I had a dilemma that I faced for a considerable period of time. I could not have a dialogue with anyone about the subject matter, except for one or two individuals who expressed genuine interest to know more. At work, I was not allowed to discuss any such topic with a coworker within the facility. I could not discuss with any of my family members because they lacked the expertise to shed any light on the subject matters. I could not openly discuss with some friends whom I knew because they would have thought that I permanently lost my mind resulting from my illness. Nobody would understand what I wanted to know. But, deep inside, I was quite restless. I desperately needed to know the Truth. I kept on praying and meditating upon the Lord daily. I also wondered often - what was the reason for His Grace upon me? I did not do anything special to deserve His Mercy. Yet I felt all along that He loved me. He showed His Compassion to me. I know He has helped and guided me through all these years. Relentlessly, all along I prayed for His Guidance and asked Him to show me the Truth and the Way. And, He did!

He answered all my prayers. Thankfully, I found the Light that I was looking for, and, gradually, I found the meaning of everything that I witnessed and much more. Through His Grace, I found my true identity in Him for which I'll remain ever grateful to Him.

This new edition is a sincere attempt for me to share my Miraculous True Experience with all my Readers, regardless of their religion, culture or background. Hopefully, this book will help many who might be confused today in this broken world and wondering, "What is the Truth?" Hopefully, they will find the meaning of life and discover their true identity. I encourage each one of my readers to seek and find Him. Once you find Him, place Him in your heart safely guarded so that you do not lose Him.

"Ask and it will be given to you; seek and you will find; knock and the door will be opened to you." – Matthew 7:7 - NIV

Gratefully,
Santosh (Sandy) Acharjee

Acknowledgements for the New Edition

This would have been an impossible task for me to write this edition of the book without the genuine love and support I received from so many. Without their help, I could not have done this. Therefore, I am indebted to all of them.

First and foremost, I must thank my Lord for His Mercy, for His Grace, and for His Blessings upon me. He is the main source of my inspiration. He is the One who asked me to write the first two books, which I have complied with and has already been accomplished. Now, I can clearly understand why He asked me to write them. He used the first two books for my own personal development and understanding of who He is as I began to grow in my relationship with Him. Now that I know who He is, He has instructed me to combine the two books into one book; this edition. This new edition is not only for me, but also for my family members and for anyone who wants to know Him and follow Him. I thank my Lord from the bottom of my heart for everything that He has done for me. Ever since my Encounter with Him, He has never left me. I feel His Presence with me always. He guides me in every step I take. I am so thankful for His Guidance. Without Him I am nothing. I cannot do anything. He is my strength. "Thank you, Lord, for your faithfulness."

The very next person I want to thank is my wife, Jharna (Janet). She has put up with a lot of my stubbornness (it proves that I am a human, and I am not perfect). But next to my Lord, she is the one I love the most. She has been a real gem to me. I have been so fortunate that God has brought her into my life. Over the years I witnessed her through the good times, as well as the bad times, but she held firm with her steady hands and proved repeatedly that her family was the most important asset in her life. She sacrificed so much for the welfare of my family quite often; many times I have forgotten to thank her. Without her loyalty and cooperation, it would have been impossible to come to this point of my life, so I say, "Thank you, Jharna, for everything."

I am also thankful to my immediate family members: my daughter, my son, my daughter-in-law, my granddaughter. "I love all of you. I want all of you to know that you make me very proud. I thank my Lord that He brought all of you into my life as His blessings. Nothing makes me happier when I see you happy and smiling. May the Lord always protect you from the hands of the evil one!

I must thank Grace Church and all their Pastors. I know Grace Church has been immensely blessed by the Lord. As a result, the power of the Holy Spirit is very noticeable, not only through the love and affection of all the Pastors, but also from the elders, members, and all staff members. I learned a lot from Pastor Jonathan Schaeffer, Pastor Steve Harper, Pastor Austin Shaw, Pastor Gregg Carrick, Pastor Jim Hicks, and all the other Pastors. "All of you are the Lord's blessings to us. Thank you all for your passion in helping others."

Especially, I must thank Pastor Steve Harper for his continued encouragement to write this edition. Steve has been a tremendous resource to bring this edition to reality. He definitely deserves special recognition. "Thank you, Steve! You are always eager to help me. I'm so thankful to you. You have been like a true brother to me."

Pastor Steve connected me with Lauraine Myers, who helped me extensively in making the entire book scripturally compliant with proper interpretations as well as in the reviewing and editing processes. Lauraine is extremely talented when it comes to reviews and edits; whether it is with texts, spellings, grammar, formatting, quotes from scriptures and their proper interpretations; she is a pro. She is not only highly knowledgeable, she is super-efficient. She is truly a multi-talented person. I am very fortunate to have Lauraine as one of my key Editors. Without her dedication and support, this book would not have been completed. "Thank you, Lauraine, for everything!"

I am also so fortunate to have two Editors for this book. The other Editor is Marilyn Neale. Marilyn has edited all of my previous editions. Marilyn's dedication and support are unquestionable. As usual, she has spent a considerable amount of time on this book in order to detect errors and mistakes. "Thank you, Marilyn!"

Also, Marilyn's husband, Ted Neale, helped me whenever I needed some advice. Ted was always there to provide me with guidance. "Thank you, Ted!"

There are a few other individuals who helped me immensely behind the scene. I thank you all!

Gratefully,
Santosh (Sandy) Acharjee

Acknowledgements for the First Book — A Miraculous True Story

There are many people who truly helped me go through my crisis period, and, without their genuine support and help, I would not be in a position to complete this book today. I need to mention some of their names and sincerely thank them all for their dedication, support, care and love.

Before I mention any names, I must sincerely thank God for His amazing love and unending mercy; for His kindness; for His loving conversation and guidance; for sending me back to the earth giving me a second chance with some specific instructions; and for His assurance to see me again next time. "Lord, please give me strength, courage, wisdom and guidance, so that I can complete my unfinished tasks prior to my next visit."

The very next person I must thank is my wife, Jharna (Janet). She has been with me in every step of my crisis period. She has been a true companion. She always tried to keep me cheered up, even though she herself was tired, nervous and scared. She spent many nights with me in the hospital, sometimes with no sleep or very little sleep. All I can say to my wife is that you are a real gem, and I have been fortunate to have you as my life partner. You have been with me in every step on this side of Heaven. You have witnessed everything from the start of the crisis to the end. While I was at the Gateway to the Kingdom of Heaven and enjoying the beautiful view of the Heaven, including a loving conversation with God there, you literally were going through the roughest time of your life, sometimes not knowing what to do. I am sorry for all the events and I sincerely thank you for everything that you did for me.

I also must thank all my immediate family members who took much time from their work and spent a considerable amount of time visiting me in the hospital and taking care of one another.

I also would like to thank all of the doctors, nurses, nursing assistants, patient care assistants and technicians who took care of me during the entire crisis period. I would like to name a few doctors for their total dedication.

They are: Dr. M. D., Dr. U. K., Dr. P. V., Dr. J. L., Dr. P. C., Dr. D. H., Dr. A. S., Dr. J. S., Dr. M. L., Dr. E. S., Dr. J. S, Dr. G. H, Dr. J. M., Dr. L. Q., Dr. R. G., Dr. R. F., Dr. P. A., Dr. K. P, Dr. B. E., Dr. S. C. and Dr. V. N.

Thank you all. Without your dedication and utmost care, I would not be able to get better again, standing on my feet and ultimately writing this book.

I need to thank all of the nurses and other health care teams at the Intensive Care Unit on the upper floor, as well as all the super nurses and other professionals at the Critical Care Unit of the CVICU. I can still remember a few of their names such as Kelly, Kristen, Julianne, Rita, Mary Jo, Bogusia, Cathy, Pat, etc, etc. Every one of them was outstanding. I remember a few of the support team members such as Missy and Dan. Especially, I need to thank Dan, who is a patient care assistant at the CVICU. Dan always went an extra mile out of his way in order to help me. I also need to thank Steve who is a R.N. at the CVICU. Steve was very helpful to me and to my wife. Steve worked very diligently to bring me back to life. Thanks to all of you. Please forgive me if I cannot remember all of your names.

I need to thank all my colleagues, my bosses, my friends, who always supported me throughout the crisis. Many of them visited me on a regular basis to show their supports. "A friend in need is a friend indeed." They are truly my friends. I need to mention some of their names.

They are Frank and Ann DiTomasso, Regis and Marilyn Minerd, Joe and Ann Marie Mezzina, Al Jerele, David Stech, Kelly Grudzinski, John Higgs, Ted and Marilyn Neale, Bud Koller and many others.

As far as encouraging me to start writing the first book, a few people have continuously suggested that I do so. They are, George Cantley, Ted Neale and his wife, Marilyn Neale.

As far as from the start to completion of this book is concerned, one person has supported me the most. She is Marilyn Neale. She has spent many hours in reviewing and editing the texts; guiding me in every step;

suggesting alternate words; and making several phone calls to potential publishers and other organizations.

Marilyn, you have been like a true sister to me. You were always keeping an eye for any potential pitfalls when you edited the book. Without your continued guidance and support, this book would not have been completed and published. Thank you very much.

There are many others who encouraged me to write the first book and helped me in various ways. I am thankful for their guidance and support. I apologize for not mentioning all of their names.

Sincerely,
Santosh (Sandy) Acharjee

Introduction Of The First Book

I have never written a book in my life thus far nor have I ever had any intentions to write one at any time. I do not consider myself a scholar, since I am not one. I am just a typical ordinary person.

But I do consider myself a strong family-oriented person; since my family has always been very important to me. I have always tried my best to fulfill my family's needs as much as possible. I always wanted the best for them within my means.

I have never been a strong religious person, abiding by any strict rules. However, I have always maintained good moral values to myself and my family. I was born a Hindu, and my father was always a very strong orthodox Hindu. He was a well renowned Sanskrit scholar, as well as a part-time Hindu priest. I did not step into my father's profession. I chose a different career path.

Although I myself was never a strong religious follower of any faith, I always believed in the existence of God from my childhood since I was raised in a conservative Hindu family environment.

As a student, I quickly understood that nothing in the world just happened on its own. Nothing comes into existence unless someone makes it or someone somehow is responsible for the action.

For example, each and every person in the whole world, we did not come on our own. Our parents had to create us. Look at the three basic necessities for our survival - we need food, shelter and clothes to survive. Do they come on their own? They do not come on their own - someone had to make them. We live in some form of dwelling - they do not come on their own. Many people are behind the creation before we can live in our dwelling. Our clothes do not come on their own - someone had to create them. In the same manner, we can look at everything in the whole world, and we will find that nothing came on its own - Someone is or was responsible behind its creation.

I became a manufacturing engineer by profession. Throughout my career, my job basically was to create more complex, precise, challenging, and various shaped components. And at the end, when I looked at the final product, I asked myself - "How did they get here? Did they come on their own?" Of course not - there were many "creators" behind them.

My childhood belief in the existence of God at some point changed to the status of God as a Creator, and I became convinced that nothing in the world came on its own. Someone had to create each and every item in the whole world. This earth, the beautiful mountains, the enormous oceans, the rain forests, the atmosphere, and the changing seasons (whatever we see or we do not see) all had to be created by Someone. They did not come on their own.

Beyond this earth, the sun, the moon, the planetary systems, the entire universe had to be created by a Master Creator.

In my profession, we always strive for three things: quality, craftsmanship and low cost. Whenever we create something, these three factors are always the common attributes. In my life thus far, I have traveled extensively throughout many parts of the world, and every time I see the magnificent creation work of the Master Creator, I am amazed by the superb quality and flawlessness of the master craftsmanship. I often wondered if there was the third factor - namely, the cost. The third factor is most likely only limited to us as human beings.

As I grew older, sometimes I would wonder about the purpose of our life here on earth. We are born; we live here for x number of years; and then suddenly one day we die. What happens after that? According to Hindu beliefs, we come back to this earth over and over again, until our soul is purified to the state that it can be united with the Divine Great Soul. Once that happens, we are permanently liberated from the revolving cycles of life and death. As I said earlier, I was never a strong religious person of any faith. Therefore, I never paid much attention to this subject, and life continued for me with normal ups and downs.

I had absolutely no clue what I had in store for a period of approximately six to eight weeks, starting on October 15, 2006. During this period, I went from a relatively healthy condition to my sudden death or near death condition, without any warning, coming right out of the blue. All the odds were against me for my survival or a slight reversal of the condition. There was no remedy available to cure the root problem. One after another my situations were getting further complicated, to the point that I had to experience my death or near death condition. It happened on October 21, 2006.

From the beginning of this trauma, I always felt that an Invisible Force was causing everything, and none of us had any control over the situation.

Then, quite unexpectedly, I met God in person at the Gateway to the Kingdom of Heaven.

Initially, I was tremendously nervous and shaky by seeing the huge, gigantic-sized figure of God. But soon I discovered how kind, how loving and a genuine friend He was.

I had a heart-to-Heart conversation with God for some time. He graciously sent me back to the earth and asked me to complete my unfinished tasks until He sees me again.

This book is one of the unfinished tasks that He asked me to complete.

He asked me to write the Truth and share the Truth with everyone without any fear.

He also asked me not to keep one penny from the sales of this book for myself. Each and every penny earned from the sales of this book must be spent to help the poor.

This book is about my experience; how it started; how things happened; and how miraculously I bounced back to life again.

This is a true story, and the writing of this book is fully inspired by God Himself. I tried my best to write everything in its truest form. I felt His presence was guiding me whenever I was writing this book.

As I said earlier, I am not a scholar. I am strictly an average person. By the same token, I am also not a professional writer. I have never written a book in my life nor did I have any intention to write one now. I apologize to all my readers for any errors or mistakes found in this book.

Also, I am not a Theologian. I have never been a strong religious follower of any faith.

I consider myself to be an extremely fortunate person to be able to eyewitness the Kingdom of Heaven; to find the one and only narrow Entry Door to Heaven; and to meet God in person. I am extremely thankful to God that He sent me back to the earth with some specific instructions and tasks.

Regardless of what religion or faith to which we belong. The truth is: there is One, and only One, God - the Master Craftsman, the Master Creator of the entire universe. It does not matter by what name we call Him. He remains the same as One and only Supreme Being.

He loves all of us equally. There is no reason for Him to love me any more than you. I have not done anything special for Him to deserve that favor.

Sudden Crisis In Life

The date was October 15, 2006 and the day was Sunday. As I arose from my bed in the morning, I looked through my bedroom window and I said to myself, "What a beautiful morning it is! The sun is shining and the temperature looks perfect for a typical fall day - not too cold, not too warm."

I kept thinking that it won't be long before the cold weather gets here; and we are not going to have very many days like this one before the winter sets in. Therefore, I decided to enjoy the day, starting with a healthy breakfast in company with my near and dear ones.

Little did I know about the outcome of that gorgeous morning with a healthy breakfast plan. The beautiful morning quickly turned into a hellish one, as one of my near and dear family members suddenly attacked another near and dear one for no apparent reason. I would not have believed it if it did not happen in front of my eyes. I always regarded all of my family members as loving, caring and understanding individuals. Frankly speaking, I was in a total shock.

This unexpected situation totally marred the morning, and its effect ruined the entire day causing undue heartaches for myself and my loved ones. Someday, I intend to write another book stressing the absolute necessity of peace and harmony within the family members. Lack of peace and harmony among the family members is undoubtedly destroying many families in our society. At the moment, not much is done to understand the root causes and to take positive remedial actions.

That particular day could have been one of the most enjoyed as well as cherished days in my life. But what we think and expect does not always seem to happen.

There is a saying in English, "Man proposes. God disposes." The most beautiful morning for me undoubtedly ended as one of the worst days in my life. It seemed that some invisible power was causing the events of the day, and I had no control over any of the situations that led one thing to another. I felt myself as someone totally helpless with absolutely no power.

However, time does not wait for anyone. The day passed, and soon the night fell. My beloved wife and I were deeply moved by the unexpected events of the day. Neither she nor I had any appetite for having food or drinks - we simply did not feel like eating anything for our dinners. But the next morning was Monday, and we arose early to go to work. Therefore, we had to eat something just to survive. After dinner, we went to bed, but both of us could not sleep for quite some time, since we were preoccupied with the events of the day.

I did not know exactly when I dozed off, but later in the night I woke up with a pain in my upper stomach and abdomen. This was a sharp pain, and I never had experienced a similar type of pain before. Considering the day was quite eventful, hectic and having an unwilling dinner that evening which might have caused the indigestion and, therefore, the pain. I took one Rolaids (Antacid) tablet with a glass of water. After a few minutes, the pain seemed to ease, and I went back to sleep again.

The next morning (October 16), I woke up as usual and prepared myself for work. My wife insisted that I make an appointment with a physician who is a specialist in internal organs to find out why I had the severe pain at night. I nodded and left home for work.

That morning, I called Dr. P. V.'s office. Dr. P. V. is an internal organs specialist whom I met a few months earlier. Dr. P. V.'s secretary kindly gave me an appointment for the early afternoon. After a general check-up, the doctor asked me to go to the nearest hospital lab next morning, since he arranged for an immediate ultra sound test of my liver, gall bladder, pancreas and duodenum. The doctor also advised me to check into the nearest hospital should the pain return.

The night of October 16, I did not have any pain. When I awoke in the morning of October 17, I said to myself, "Everything must be fine. The pain must have been caused due to stress and indigestion."

However, since I had an appointment for various lab tests in the morning I went straight to the nearest hospital lab and had all the tests done. I asked the lab technician when my test results would be known.

The technician said that the results would be sent to Dr. P. V. in three to four days.

After completing the lab tests, I went back to my work. I did not feel anything unusual. I kept saying to myself, "Everything must be fine and the pain must have been from the indigestion. There could be nothing serious." But deep inside I was still curious to know the results of my ultra sound tests. I called Dr. P. V.'s office and asked if they would call me and let me know when they received the test results. They said, "It will take a few more days, and the doctor will definitely contact you."

I went home after work, had my dinner, briefly watched TV, played a few computer games, and went to bed around 10:30 PM.

Shortly before midnight on October 17, I awoke with a very severe pain in my upper stomach and abdomen. The pain was taking place in the same area as it happened a few nights earlier. I got up and took a Rolaids tablet, as I had done a few nights earlier. Last time, a few minutes after taking the Rolaids, I was feeling better. This time, it was just the opposite. My pain was going to the extreme. It felt as if someone was stabbing me with a sharp knife over and over. It was beyond description. As the night was progressing, so was my pain worsening. I could not control myself and started to moan and groan.

My unexplained moaning and groaning awoke my wife. She tried to calm me down, but the pain was going far beyond my tolerance level. I felt my heart was racing and had an irregular beat. I could not lie down; I could not sit down; I could not stand up - what a terrible situation! I felt the pain was now spreading towards my chest.

My breathing was getting very irregular, and I was sweating profusely. By this time, it felt as if someone had changed the knife from a small one to a large one and started stabbing me left and right with the larger knife. I've never experienced anything like this in my life. Neither could I imagine that a pain of this type ever existed.

The time was a few minutes past 2 AM (October 18, early morning). By then, both my wife and I were beginning to wonder if I was having a heart attack. We knew whatever was happening, it was quite serious, and it required immediate medical attention. We grabbed the phone and desperately dialed 911 for immediate help. As the minutes passed, my condition was worsening. At this time, I found it very difficult to breathe, although I could hear the siren of the ambulance from a distance speeding towards its destination. The siren stopped as the ambulance parked in front of our house.

Quite hastily, two members of the paramedics came in the house and transferred me from my house to the ambulance. They found my pulse rate was abnormally high. My blood pressure was also dangerously high. They gave me a number of baby aspirins and asked me to swallow them. They also suspected that I was most likely having a heart attack.

The nearest hospital from my house is approximately four miles away. The paramedics called the Emergency Department of the hospital and advised them of my condition. They asked my wife to join them. One member of the paramedics was monitoring my condition during the transit, while the other drove the vehicle.

As soon as the ambulance pulled into the emergency area, they rapidly admitted me and put me in the Intensive Care Unit. The date of admittance was October 18, 2006, and the local time was approximately 3 AM.

Further Complications At ICU

In the hospital, I was immediately given an I.V. Soon I was put on the breathing machine. I was also hooked up to the vital monitoring system. I was told to lie down at all times, not to get up for any reason since my pulse rate was extremely high at 202. The normal pulse rate is about 72.

The nurse said that they would schedule various tests as soon as the doctors arrive in the morning. She said that the doctors had been alerted of my condition. My family physician, Dr. M. D., is also associated with this hospital and he comes here on a regular basis.

I must wait until the doctors arrive to find out what is happening with me. My wife, who accompanied me to the hospital, said she would stay until the doctors arrived. She kept me a good company. I looked at the room. This room is shared with another patient, who was awake. He told me his name, but I cannot remember now. I asked him what brought him to the hospital. I believe he said it had something to do with his breathing, possibly pneumonia, but I'm not sure today what he said exactly. All I remember is that he was to be released that day, and he was anxious to go home. He had been in the hospital for a number of days.

Soon the daylight was breaking, and it was time for the shift change. New faces started to come in and introduce themselves. The lab technician came in to draw blood; patient care assistants came in to do the routine vital checks; and there were others.

I'm not sure if I was given some pain killers or not. My pain was still there, but, it was not as fatal as before. There were also a number of other people coming in and checking me, practically asking me the same questions over and over. I never met them before; therefore, I did not know who they were.

Soon Dr. M. D. came to see me. Dr. M. D. has been my family physician ever since he started his practice in Ohio. I was so happy to see him. He asked me all sorts of questions. He said that they did not know what was wrong with me. They would perform a variety of tests, including CT scan, MRI, blood tests, x-rays, etc., to determine the cause. My wife said that I had done the ultra sound tests in the same hospital just a day earlier, and we were still waiting to know the results. Dr. M. D. said that he would look into it. He started to check me with his stethoscope and I could tell from his face that he was deeply concerned. He said my pulse rate was extremely high, and I must not get up for any reason. As he left the room, he said he would be back as soon as the diagnosis was completed. That was Wednesday, October 18, 2006.

I was taken downstairs to various labs for several tests, including a CT scan. My wife accompanied me everywhere. I asked her to go home and rest for a while, but she refused. She said that she would not be able to rest at home leaving me in this situation, since she would be worried about the outcome.

It was a busy day as I was undergoing various types of tests. There were also other doctors who were coming in and asking me various questions. The day passed with tests and anxieties. I still did not know what was wrong with me.

My daughter came to visit me in the evening. When the visiting hours were over, I insisted that my wife go home and rest for a while. Otherwise, both of us would be in the hospital. It was hard enough just to have one person being sick. If both of us became sick, the situation would be entirely out of control. She went home reluctantly and said that she would be back in the morning.

After my wife and daughter went home, I noticed that my room-mate was still there. I mentioned to him that I thought he would be going home that day. He said that he would be released the next day. We chatted for a while, until at some point, I dozed off.

Whether I dozed off due to exhaustion or medication, I do not know. I kept waking up as the technicians came to draw blood, check on vitals or check my blood sugar level, since I am diabetic. They did not care whether I was asleep or awake. They had to attend to their duties.

However, these interruptions kept me from sleeping. Once the sleep was interrupted, it was difficult to sleep again. Even when I managed to sleep again, there was the next interruption - breathing therapy. I had to do the therapy three or four times a day until the medication depleted each time. It usually took about 15 minutes to deplete the medication. Then there were the breathing exercises - I had to do it four or five times per day. I am not complaining as I know all these treatments are absolutely necessary and, without these treatments, a patient in my condition cannot get better.

The night passed on. Now, it was Thursday, October 19, 2006. My wife could not sleep well at home because of the anxieties. She came to see me early in the morning. My daughter dropped her off at the hospital on her way to work that morning. The situation did not change. We still did not know what was happening to me. Routine tests and diagnoses continued.

I cannot remember what time it was when Dr. M. D. came to see me. He said that he had some good news and some bad news. The good news is that they know what is happening, but the bad news is they cannot do anything to rectify it. I asked him to elaborate the good news. He said that I had a severe gall bladder attack. During the attack, several gall stones ruptured, and it appeared that they ruptured with a tremendous force. A few stones penetrated the nearby organ, pancreas, and went from one end to the other. The pancreas was punctured causing it to bleed, and that was making the heart work overtime, resulting in an extremely high pulse rate condition.

He said, "Your heart rate is 202. The situation is very serious." He also added, "In medical terms, it is called pancreatic, but, in your case, you have the pancreas that is severely wounded and damaged. A situation that is not normal."

I asked Dr. M. D., if anything can be done to rectify the problem, and he said to me, "That is the bad news. We can remove the gall bladder surgically, but we cannot proceed until your pulse rate normalizes.

The doctor continued, "Your pulse rate will not be normalized until the pancreas is healed."

The doctor paused for a moment and continued, "This is the dilemma. There is absolutely nothing we can do about the damaged pancreas. As of now, there are no medications or surgical procedures available to repair the ruptured pancreas."

He continued, "Medical science can only do the pancreas transplant, but in your case that is also not feasible. First, we must find a donor organ, and then have the proper surgical condition."

I asked Dr. M. D., "What do you mean by proper surgical condition?"

The doctor said, "With the current heart rate condition that you have, we cannot even do a gall bladder removal operation. Gall bladder operation is considered to be a relatively simple operation. If we cannot do a simple gall bladder operation, how can we do a major pancreas transplant operation? It is very risky, and we will not do it."

Dr. M. D. stayed in the room a few more minutes and said he was sorry that medically nothing can be done to ease the situation. He said, "The only thing you can do is pray and hope for the condition to improve so that we can at least remove the gall bladder and possibly some stones."

He checked my vitals and left the room with instructions to the appropriate personnel for a 24-hour, around-the-clock intensive care services.

After Dr. M. D. left, both my wife and I were saddened to know the diagnosis. Both of us had been eagerly waiting to hear some positive news. Now, we knew what was wrong with me, but there were no solutions, no remedies.

How would the wounded pancreas get healed? The doctor said I was having internal bleeding due to the puncture of the pancreas caused by the penetrating gall stones. There were no medications to make me better, and the doctors could not do any surgical procedures due to my abnormally high pulse rate.

How would I get better? Worries and concerns surrounded me. My roommate wished me well and left the hospital, as he was released. I kept thinking, "When would I be released? When would I be able to go home? Perhaps, that day would never come."

My wife kept cheering me up, giving me hope and saying, "Don't worry, everything will be ok." But deep inside, both she and I knew it would be a long time before everything would be ok, perhaps never.

I remember a number of doctors who started visiting me and checking my conditions with genuine concern. I also remember some of their names, Dr. P. V., Dr. U. K., Dr. V. N. and a few more. They basically said the same thing as Dr. M. D. had said to me earlier: they could not do anything until my pulse rate came down; the situation was pretty serious and they asked me to hang in.

My daughter came to visit me in the evening. I insisted that my wife go home and take some rest. I told her not to worry about me, and I'd be fine. She reluctantly left with mixed emotions. On one hand she knew the cause of my problems; on the other hand, she was very concerned to know that there was no remedy.

After she left, I felt the room was quieter than the night before. I realized that might be due to the departure of my roommate. I could not sleep. I kept thinking of the events of the day. I was still hoping that I might be able to go back to my normal life someday. But right now I could not see how it was possible. "The doctors will not even operate on my gall bladder to remove the ruptured stones. They are still floating inside somewhere. How will my wounded pancreas get healed?" I was desperately searching for a ray of hope, but I did not find any.

Needless to say, I did not sleep well that night, since I passed the night amidst anxieties, pain and uncertainties. The next morning was Friday, October 20, 2006. For some reason, I was finding it difficult to breathe, as if some heavy load was resting on my chest. As usual, my wife came in the early morning. She did not sleep well either. She was also concerned about the remedy or lack of remedy in this situation.

When the RN came to see me, I mentioned about my difficulty in breathing. The doctor was notified, and I was sent for more tests. When I was brought back to my room, I asked my wife if she would help me to the attached bathroom. I had been bed-ridden ever since I came to the hospital, and it would probably do me good to stand up. She hesitated and wanted to call the RN. I said not to bother them. "They are busy, and I'm not the only patient." She did not want to do that, since the doctor previously told me not to stand up. I told her I'd be fine. "Let's try." Reluctantly she helped me to stand up.

This was the first time I was standing since I was brought to the hospital. Actually, I felt proud of being able to stand again and being able to walk to the attached bathroom. I looked at the mirror in the bathroom - my beard was growing big, and I should shave it off. My wife said, "Don't bother. Let the beard grow."

At that time, I saw the floor RN came rushing into the room and speaking to me in an extremely angry voice. She wanted to know what exactly I was doing and why did I stand up. I tried to explain. She quickly placed me in my bed and said to me, "Absolutely no standing! It is an order!"

I asked her why she was doing this. She said that when I stood up in the bathroom, my pulse rate went so high that I could have collapsed any moment.

I asked her how she knew that. She said that she could monitor my heart rate from her office twenty four hours around the clock. She left the room asking my wife to keep an eye on me so that I did not stand up again.

That was the end of my adventure of standing up for a long time, but I was still feeling good being able to stand up, even though the duration was extremely short.

Later, I was advised by one of the doctors that the tests taken earlier that day indicated I had pneumonia. I asked the doctor what caused my pneumonia. The doctor said it was not uncommon to have pneumonia in the hospital, "It could be viral."

Having pneumonia was the reason I was having trouble breathing. The doctor said that I had some fluids in both of my lungs and it would take a few more tests to determine which lung needed to be drained first.

This news had shocked both me and my wife. Now, it seems to be one thing after another. This one is quite unexpected and out of the blue. However, breathing is a very basic need for survival. If we cannot breathe, we cannot live much longer.

My situation was getting more and more complex: first the ruptured gall stones, which are still floating; the surgeons are unable to do a simple surgery to remove the gall bladder and stones; a punctured and wounded pancreas that was still under shock and unable to do any remedial action for that; now the viral pneumonia, having fluids in both lungs and much difficulty in breathing. I was wondering, "What would be the next?"

I was taken downstairs for a few more tests, one of which was an MRI to determine the amount of fluid and its exact locations. I was advised that the doctor will perform a simple surgical procedure next day (Saturday, October 21, 2006) around noon. I would need to be brought down a little earlier so that the doctors could do a final review of the condition prior to the operation.

As usual, my daughter came to visit me in the evening. My wife went home reluctantly. I asked her to contact my son, who lived in the neighboring state of Michigan, and let him know of this new development.

After my wife left, I felt very sad and anxious. I kept thinking, "I did not come to the hospital for this treatment. I came here to find out and fix the cause of my original pains."

The doctors had been saying that they could not do anything about my original problem, and now I was going to be treated for pneumonia that I did not have when I came to the hospital. It seemed that the odds were against me. An unknown force had taken control of my destiny, and I was totally helpless.

But my wife kept cheering me up; she continued to encourage me. She said, "We must go with what the doctors are saying. The doctors know better, and they are here to make the patients better."

Death Or Near Death Experience

The night passed. It was now Saturday, October 21, 2006. I dozed off a few times throughout the night, and every time I woke up whenever the routine check-up people were conducting their duties. As usual, my wife came in the morning. She also did not sleep well.

I was taken down a little earlier than the scheduled time for my fluid draining operation. I was brought down to the MRI lab where the procedure was going to take place. My wife came along.

I sat on a bed exposing my back towards the MRI technician. The attending RN explained the procedure to me - they were going to drain the fluid out of my left lung. The doctor, who was going to perform the surgical procedure, was Dr. X. He came in and put a needle on the left side of my back. He said that it would take a few minutes before the needle would locally numb the area and he would be back in a few minutes.

I noticed that there seemed to be a little difference of opinion between the nurse, the MRI technician and the doctor with the amount of fluid or its exact location. I was not able to find out what exactly was the cause for the difference of opinion.

The doctor took his time to return to the lab. When he came, he took a long needle and penetrated it through my back into my lungs. I immediately felt pain during the procedure and asked the RN if it was supposed to hurt? She and the doctor said, "A little." But to me it seemed to hurt more than 'a little.'

I could not see my back. My wife later said there was hardly any fluid that came out. It was a very little amount of fluid mixed with blood. After the procedure, they took me next door for an x-ray and sent me upstairs.

I knew something was terribly wrong, as I started to feel extremely unwell immediately after the operation. But I did not know exactly what was wrong with me. I asked the attending RN if my post operation x-ray was normal. She said to me, "Everything is fine."

Once I was taken back up to my room, I saw that my son, my daughter-in-law and my granddaughter were waiting for me there. I was very happy to see them. The last time I saw them was on the previous Sunday, October 15, 2006.

I believe by then the time was shortly after 1 PM. This was the first time I noticed that, deep inside me, an inner voice started telling me that my life was coming to an end very soon, probably in less than 30 to 45 minutes. The inner voice continued to warn me, as my departure time from this world was getting nearer by the minutes.

I kept thinking that it takes usually over three hours by car from my son's place to the hospital. I asked him if they had lunch.

They said, "No."

I told them to go and have something quick in the cafeteria downstairs, for two reasons, one that the cafeteria stops serving lunch at 1:30 PM. The other was I felt tired and I needed to take a few minutes rest. I also told them not to delay in returning, as I needed to see them back as soon as possible.

They complied and went downstairs. My wife also went with them. Up until now, my wife was trying to cope with all the difficult situations by herself. Seeing my son, my daughter-in-law and my granddaughter there gave her some strength and moral support that she needed very badly.

But the real truth of my sending them away was that I knew my life was coming to an end very soon. If something happened in the next few minutes, they probably would remain hungry without food, as they would have no appetite for food should I pass away. I did not want them to stay hungry after a long drive from their home.

I was feeling weaker by the minute. The inner voice continued to tell me, "Your life is over, only a few more minutes left for you to live."

I was anxiously waiting for my loved ones to return to the room. I did not want to depart from this world without saying farewell to them.

Around that time, they returned to the room and saw me awake. They were asking if I slept a little or not. I told them, "Listen, I need to tell you something. I've only a few more minutes to live in this world. There is something terribly wrong with me."

My wife and my son said, "Don't say anything like this. You will be fine. Everything will be ok."

I said to them, "I do not have much time. Let me say it before it is too late. These are the final moments of my life."

I begged them to live peacefully and in harmony after my departure. I asked them to take care of each other. I blessed them with my final blessings and wished them well.

At that point, I looked at my wife, and I took her hand in mine. I said to her, "I might not have been an easy person to live with for all these years we had been together. Please forgive me for any and all of my wrong doings."

I continued to say that I loved her, and I loved the family dearly, and I was sorry to leave her in this manner. I repeatedly urged all of them to live in peace and in harmony. I blessed them all.

My wife and son still did not realize what I was trying to say. They kept on saying, "You'll be fine! Why are you saying such things? You'll be fine!" I told them again, "Listen, I only have a few moments of my life left. Good bye to all of you, and God bless you! Love one another and stay in peace."

My wife looked at me, and, for the first time since the beginning of this trauma, I saw tears in her eyes. She realized that I was serious and not joking. Whatever I was saying was genuine and urgent. She said to me, "You cannot leave me like this alone."

I said, "I'm sorry. I didn't plan it this way either. But the time has come for me to say Goodbye! I love you!" I touched her forehead and tendered my final blessings!

Within a few seconds, I collapsed on the bed and they said later to me that my body was getting stiff. My wife didn't know what to do or say. The entire episode was so sudden and unexpected, that it did not sink in for a few moments.

Either she or my son pushed the emergency call button for help. The RN for that floor rushed into the room, and she was shocked to see me die that quickly.

She realized what was going on. She immediately declared, "*Code Blue! Room #____*" on me and asked for the Emergency Response Team to rush into that Room. Later I found out that the "*Code Blue or Code 99*" is a secret code used by the hospital to alert the Emergency Response Team that someone is passing away or just passed away.

After I collapsed, I felt all my senses were disappearing one by one very quickly. First, I lost my visual sense - I could not see anyone. I was talking to them a few moments earlier. Now I could not talk. My wife was holding my hand. Very soon, I lost the sense of touch. I lost the other senses, as well. But I felt that my sense of hearing was still there for some time. Several minutes after collapsing, I was still able to hear what was being said in the room.

If I may offer a suggestion to my readers at this point, please do not say any negative words or comments at the time of someone's death. You may think he or she is dead and what you are saying he or she cannot hear. You'll be surprised to know that the sense of hearing is the last one that departs at the time of death. You do not want to make comments or say something that you would not normally say in front of the person if the person was alive.

In my case, I could not see, I could not feel the touch, I could not smell nor could I speak, but I continued to hear the noises of several medical professionals rushing into the room, asking everyone to leave the room in a hurry. They were trying very hard to revive me, but, by their words, I could sense that they were not succeeding. I heard one doctor saying, "We are rapidly losing him" and another doctor said, "He is not responding at all. We just lost him!"

These are the last words that I could remember. I could hear them no more. All my senses seemed to fade away. Everything was quiet. I fell into a deep eternal sleep.

Journey To An Unknown Destination

For a moment, I felt like, "I do not belong to this world any more. I need to depart from here. My world is gone. I could see my body lying flat on the hospital bed. But I felt there was no reason for me to stay here anymore."

For some reason, I felt like my brain was still functioning for the analytical or reasoning point of view because I was wondering, "What do I do now? Where do I go from here? I'm no longer a part of this world."

As I was wondering, suddenly a bright Light appeared before me. The Light was extremely bright and sharp.

As soon as I saw the Light, I knew it appeared before me with superior authority. I knew, "It means business and I better obey it. One little thought of disobeying it will be very fatal."

The Light kept a safe distance from me. Then, the Light became very bright. Due to its extreme brightness, everything disappeared from me. I could not see a thing any more, other than the bright Light. The only thing I could do was to obey Its command. The Light started to pull me, and I was to follow the Light. I noticed the Light was pulling me like a magnet pulls the metal. I've absolutely no control over anything. My job was to follow the Light wherever It wants to take me.

I started to follow the Light, keeping a safe distance. The Light was bright and scary at first, but now I felt Its mission was to protect me and guide me throughout the journey to my unknown destination.

I remember following the Light, traveling at a very fast speed, faster than anything I knew. During the journey, I began to like the Light as It was protecting me.

I found the Light to be soothing. I remember passing through some black holes like big round tunnels at tremendous speed. Together, we traveled for quite some time. Exactly how long, I do not know.

After a long journey, suddenly the Light stopped, and I had to stop. If one is following a speedy car on the highway and, if the car ahead stops all of a sudden, the car behind must stop. It was a similar situation. I was following the Light, and, when It stopped, I had to stop. When the Light stopped, It was still looking at me, and I was looking at Him, as well. I was wondering, "Why did the Light stop moving? What do I do now?"

I kept on gazing at the Light from a safe distance. To me, the distance between the Light and me seemed to be a several thousand feet away.

I noticed that the Light was still gazing at me, as if it was keeping an eye on me for every move I would make.

At that point, I was beginning to wonder, "Where am I? What is this place? What's behind the Light? Why is the Light not moving? Why did it stop?"

Magnificent Beauty Of Heaven

Up until now, I couldn't see anything besides the Light. The Light was so bright, and I had been gazing at it for a considerable length of time.

Nothing else was visible to me.

Gradually, the area where the Light was situated was beginning to clear for me. For the first time, I was seeing that the Light stopped inside a large compound that was fenced in with very high and extraordinarily beautiful fences.

Slowly, I could see the entire area as far as I could see. The area was fenced in from all four sides. The area inside the fences was the most beautiful large compound I had ever seen in my life.

Nothing in this world could ever come close to the beauty of this place. The fences were tall, but they were magnificent. I was so taken by the beauty of the place inside, that I could not keep my eyes away from it. The more I saw the more curious I became, and I wanted to see more.

The brightness of the Light did not blind me any longer, rather It was shining upon the entire compound with a soothing light similar to the moon light on a full moon night only several times brighter. Because of the soothing Light shining upon the area I started to see the entire area of this huge compound very clearly.

I saw, there were many marvelous big buildings after buildings. Big buildings would be an understatement. I should say, they were mansions after mansions, and they were so gorgeous and so beautiful.

The mansions were very large in size, their structures were superb, and their roofs were of a bright golden color. Some of the mansions also had bright copper colored roofs. I've not seen anything like these mansions anywhere in the world. Throughout my life, I've traveled extensively to many countries. But the beauty of this place was unique, unlike any other beautiful places I've ever seen. Its beauty was awesome and beyond description.

I could not turn my eyes away from this magnificent place. The more I saw, the more I was getting stunningly astonished. I wanted to go inside the fences. "Where are the entrance ways to this place?" I asked myself.

I continually searched for an Entrance Way, all around the perimeters as far as I could see, but I could not find one Entrance Way that was open.

Face To Face With God In Heaven

I was wondering how I could go across the beautiful fences into the magnificent compound. I started to look all around the fences as far as I could see. I was searching for at least one entrance way to this compound. I was shocked when I noticed that the entire complex was fenced in and there was not a single entrance way that I could see anywhere throughout the perimeters as far as I could see.

The entire boundary was well protected by the angel like figures. Nobody could even dare intrude into the place. I started to look all around the perimeters again and again. There were a total of 12 marvelous gates around the perimeter. Alas, there was not a single entry or gate anywhere that was open for me to enter!

I was quite disappointed not finding any gate or entrance way that was open for me to enter into this place. I started to look deeper into the compound, and I could see many angel-like figures floating. I saw from a distance some human-like beings who could either walk or float.

The entire area inside the compound looked so peaceful and so calm that I instantly fell in love with this place. I kept thinking, "How do I get into this beautiful place? There has to be an Entrance somewhere. Where is the Entrance? How can I find the Entrance?"

As I was desperately searching for the Entrance, I noticed my companion Light was still looking at me and watching me for every move I was going to make.

Not finding an Entrance into this place, I felt sad. My focus, by then, had shifted from the inside of the beautiful compound to the place where I was standing. Suddenly, I started to wonder, "Where am I? What is this place?"

It felt like I was standing somewhere. All of my attention thus far was focused on the inside and the perimeter of the fences all around the magnificent compound. At that time I was beginning to wonder, "What is this place upon which I'm standing?" My focus now shifted to the area where I was standing.

I noticed I was standing on a platform. I also noticed that I was standing at the extreme far left-hand corner, almost to the edge of this platform. For the first time, I realized that the Light I followed all along was now situated inside the beautiful compound, and I was standing on a platform outside the compound. I also noticed that the platform was rather large (approximately 1000 feet long), and it was located at a very high altitude. And there I was – at the edge, extreme far left corner of the platform.

"Why does this platform have no railings?" I was wondering, "I'm standing so close to the edge, what if I fall off the edge?"

Being curious, I looked downwards on my left from that edge, and what I saw was the most dreadful scene of my life. If I fell off the edge, I would fall an enormous depth perhaps thousands of miles deep into an unknown world that I witnessed as the most scary place. All I could see there was a deep dungeon dark world with a huge burning lake of fire. It was so frightening that I knew this fall definitely would be the final death of my life. I could not ever imagine what kind of torment would take place after the fall. Only God knows where I'd fall and what would take place there. I looked down below again on my left and I knew what I was witnessing down below it was The Hell. The Hell I witnessed was always dark, and the only light that I saw there was burning flames. I was standing at the extreme far edge on the platform with no railing, from where I could fall very easily into the dingy dungeon, and that fall would be the permanent death for me.

Just the mere thought of the fall was so scary and so frightening that I instantly moved a few steps away from the extreme edge.

I looked at my companion Light one more time, and I noticed the Light was carefully watching me and my every move.

At that point I just realized that the magnificent place I was looking at all along was nothing but the Kingdom of Heaven, and I was standing outside the Kingdom of Heaven on a platform or an altar. As I could see some angels and some human like persons inside the compound, I desperately started to look at their faces to see if I could see a familiar face, such as my mother or my father or someone else whom I knew. I could not see anyone I recognized. I was quite disappointed by not seeing any familiar faces.

(It is worth mentioning here for the benefit of my readers that our vision works completely differently out there than they do here. Here on earth, our vision is quite limited. We can see only so far, and that view has to be without any obstruction. If there is a wall or any other obstruction that blocks the view, we cannot see what is beyond the obstruction. At the same time, if we see some people at a great distance we cannot recognize their faces, not until, they come within our viewing ranges. Over there, we will not have any such limitations. We can see very clearly what is on the other side, even if the view is obstructed by walls, or any other object. We can also see very far. The distance is not a factor at all. At the same time, when we see someone far away, our vision has the capability of zooming in on their faces, just like a very powerful camera.)

I now decided to survey the altar where I was standing on the platform at the extreme far left corner. There was no other person on the altar at the time; I was the only one.

For the first time, I started to look towards my front. The altar was approximately 200 feet wide. I noticed, at the end, towards the center, there were three big steps. Each step was about five to seven feet high, with the same depth. On top of the second step, the third step had approximately 20 to 30 feet depth and no height to it. Behind that there was a wall that was approximately 70 feet high. This back wall adjoined the boundary fences of the Kingdom of Heaven that I was looking at earlier.

I started to look from there towards my right. As I mentioned earlier, the altar was approximately 1000 feet long. As I was looking towards the center of this high walled platform, my eyes were struck in awe at what I saw. At the center of that location there was a huge throne. Lo and behold! There was the Lord! The Lord was sitting on the throne!

Loving God & The Narrow Door

As soon as I saw Him, I knew He was the Supreme Lord! I started to tremble with fear! He was so huge. Here, I am 5'6" tall standing at the extreme far left corner and looking at the center of that altar, and He was approximately 600 feet away from me. He was sitting on the throne, and at that sitting position He appeared to be approximately 35 to 40 feet tall. Therefore, when He stands up, I presume, He would be about 70 feet tall. He was very well proportioned and wore a white robe.

Seeing His huge, gigantic appearance I again started to tremble with fear. My knees felt very weak and they automatically bowed down to Him. I was standing at the extreme far edge of the platform, and I could very easily fall off the edge with my fearful trembling. He was such a powerful, overwhelming and mesmerizing figure that I could not look at Him for too long. I looked at His Face only once and I could not look at Him the second time. I was trembling with fear so much thinking that this would be the end of my life. The Lord will not spare me as I committed many sins in my life.

I could not look at Him straight at His face. I was so afraid. I continually looked at His Feet begging for His Mercy and pleading for His Forgiveness. I kept repeating the same words over and over again, 'Lord, please forgive me for my sins, Lord, please have mercy upon me.' That was a genuine repentance seeking His Forgiveness and seeking His Mercy. As I was continuously looking at His Feet, I started to look slightly towards the left of the throne (right from my position) and I was totally amazed to discover a very narrow door. The door was so narrow that it struck me as completely out of proportion.

I now realized that this narrow door is the only entrance way to the inside of the Kingdom of Heaven. All the other 12 magnificent Gates were closed. This is the only entrance way in the entire perimeter of the compound that was open for me. This is the entrance I had been desperately searching for a bit earlier.

"How can I go through this door?" I asked myself. The Lord is so giant and frightening. He is sitting near the door. I cannot dare myself to go near the door. It was quite evident to me that I could not even try to enter through the door unless the Lord allowed me to go through the door.

It had been pretty clear to me that I was now standing at the Gateway to the Kingdom of Heaven and I was completely at the mercy of the Lord. I was still nervous and trembling vigorously and I knew, it was just a matter of moments before I'd plunge into my final death into the lake of fire. But then the Lord spoke to me. He has a very deep, commanding voice, but, at the same time, I noticed His voice was also a loving one.

Language did not seem to be a barrier at all. When the Lord spoke, I could understand what He said in any of the languages that I know (Bengali, English, Hindi, German, Portuguese, etc). By the same token, it didn't matter in which language I responded, the Lord understood every word even before I spoke.

The Lord looked at me and asked, "What are you doing here?"

I shrugged my shoulder, meaning, "I do not know."

He said to me in an authoritative, but loving, voice, "Your time has not come yet. I'm sending you back to the earth. Go back until your time comes."

By then, I gathered a little courage, as I noticed I was not shaking any longer with fear. The Lord continued, "Go back and complete your unfinished tasks. When you are back I want you to love your family and love your children. Pay attention to your daughter. She needs your help."

Hearing the loving and caring voice of the Lord, I gathered a little more courage, and I asked, "Lord! I'm not worthy of standing before You. I'm a sinner! I've sinned, Lord! How can I be sure that I can enter through this narrow door next time? And, Lord, please tell me - when will be my next time?"

The Lord did not respond.

I continued to plead, "Lord! Please provide me with some guidance. How can I prepare myself for the next time? How can I make myself worthy of standing before you next time? And, I do not know how much time I'll have before the next time."

The Lord still did not respond.

I continued pleading, "Please Lord! Please guide me to prepare myself for next time. Please tell me if I need to join any church, any temple, any synagogue, any religious institute, any religious association or any other place. I'll do whatever You say, but please guide me."

The Lord looked at me and said, "No, it is not necessary for you to join any church, any temple or anything else. Those things are not important to Me."

I must admit that I was totally shocked to hear this from the Lord. All along I was under the assumption that any person who was very much involved with a church, temple, mosque, synagogue or any other religious institute they must be very religious people and, therefore, very close to God. But, God Himself is saying that these things are not important to Him.

Although the Lord indicated to me that membership to any religious group is not necessary to enter the Kingdom of Heaven, we, as humans, definitely need a support group to help us through our difficult times, remind us of the importance of worshiping God, teach us in the Ways of the Lord, and assist us in accomplishing His directives.

The Lord continued, "What is important to Me is your personal relationship with Me, how sincere, how honest, how true are you with Me? That's the only thing that counts."

I continuously looked at the Lord's feet and begged Him to be merciful to me. I said, "Lord! I am a human being. When I go back, I'll be involved with my day-to-day activities, and I'll be back to my worldly life. Please, Lord! Please give me some specific instructions or guidelines that I can follow."

Initially, the Lord didn't respond. After repeated pleadings and crying out to Him for His Guidance, the Lord looked at me and said, "Here are some instructions for you. I want you to follow them between now and your next time."

He gave me five instructions and asked me to go back to the earth until He sees me again next time.

I will elaborate on His instructions to me towards the final chapter of this book. In the meantime, I'm now back to the earth, and let me explain my experiences back here.

Return To Earth At Critical Care Unit

I believe it was Tuesday, October 24, 2006, when I finally opened my eyes (first time since I departed from this earth on previous Saturday, October 21, 2006). I cannot remember the exact time, but I remember when I opened my eyes I saw a loving motherly- type nurse sitting beside me and looking at me. When she saw me opening my eyes, she exclaimed with joy, "There you are! You finally opened your eyes. We all are anxiously waiting for you!"

I asked her, "Where am I? What is this place?"

She said to me in a loving voice, "It is a long story, my dear. Thank God! You finally opened your eyes. You have been terribly sick. We are all working hard day and night to bring you back."

I asked the motherly lady, "How did I get here?" I told her I was there with God a few moments earlier. He was talking to me, and He said to me, "I am sending you back to the earth."

She said to me, "I believe you, but for now let me go and tell all the doctors and the nurses that you have opened your eyes. Oh! They will be so happy to hear that. They are anxiously waiting for this news. It is a miracle!"

The loving motherly type nurse left the room, and I dozed off again. Even though I was asleep, I could hear the footsteps of several people coming into my room. I think they were looking at my vitals, monitoring the numbers on the life support machine, and discussing the results among themselves. I could sense from their expressions that they were full of excitement and joy.

I was dozing off and on quite frequently that day. It did not matter whether I opened or closed my eyes, I could not stop remembering every moment of my experience at the Gateway to the Kingdom of Heaven. I was so taken by the awesome beauty of the Kingdom of Heaven, that I could not keep my mind off the place where I was a few moments earlier. God's instructions to me were ringing back in my ears over and over. His final words to me were, "I'm sending you back to the earth until I see you again next time."

Readjustment After Return

It seemed to me that all of my prior experiences in this world were totally blanked out of my mind. I could not remember anything in this world, at least for the first one or two days after my return. I was definitely somewhat disoriented the first day of my return, and my recollection of events might be slightly out of sequence. However, I do remember a few major events. Let me explain those events as I remember.

Between my frequent sleepy periods, I remember once seeing my wife who was holding my hand. I looked at her, and her face definitely looked familiar. A few moments later, I could recognize her as my wife.

She asked me if I could remember anything. I shook my head indicating, "No." I saw tears in her eyes, but these tears did not appear to be tears of her sorrow. I knew these tears were reflecting her joy. She said, "Thank God! You are back! You went away, and I was so nervous, I did not know what to do."

For the first time I noticed that I could not speak. I had no voice. She was holding a clipboard and I managed to scribble. "What happened to me? Where am I? What is this place? What am I doing here?"

She asked, "Can't you remember what happened to you last Saturday?"

I wrote, "No. What happened to me?"

She said, "After you collapsed in the Intensive Care Unit room upstairs the Emergency Response Team rushed into the room and drove us away from the room in a hurry. They tried to revive you there but they failed to bring you back to life. They were there for a very long time. We were not allowed to see what they were doing. However, some doctors decided to put you on artificial life support machine and transfer you to the Critical Care Unit with twenty-four-hour/around-the- clock care."

She continued, "This is called the Critical Care Unit of this hospital. A lot of doctors and nurses have been working very hard for the last three days to bring you back to your consciousness." She paused.

I was trying to concentrate and remember any events that took place last Saturday. I could vaguely remember that I was at the Intensive Care room when I collapsed.

My mind was still occupied with the experience that I encountered outside this world. I could remember every second of my journey, every moment of my being there, but I could not remember anything that transpired here in this hospital for the last three days.

As my wife was having discussions with me, I noticed that my hands and legs were restrained to the bed. I could not move them too much. I also noticed that I was breathing through a large diameter clear plastic hose.

I wrote on the clip board. "Why are my hands and legs tied to the bed? Why am I breathing through the plastic hoses?"

She said, "Your hands and legs are restrained for your own safety so that you could not pull any of the pipes out of your body. Pulling any of the hoses or pipes could prove to be very fatal."

I wrote. "Did you say pipes? How many pipes are there?"

Before she answered I remember a nurse came into my room and asked me to take it easy. She did not want me to get over exhausted. She did not want me to get excited as it might put undue stress to my respiratory system.

My wife asked the nurse, "He wants to know how many pipes are attached to his body and what are they for."

The nurse said, "Quite a few."

She pointed her finger to one of them and said, "This large diameter hose is for your breathing. It is tied to the artificial breathing machine. All your breathing is taking place through this machine."

She continued, "You have three tubes coming off the left side of your chest. They are called drain tubes."

She said, "You have another one coming off a little below, and it is called Catheter. That is to protect your kidney."

The nurse continued, "You have intra-venous tubes feeding your body with the necessary fluids and nutrition. You also have a tube for blood transfusion."

My wife commented, "Pulling any of the tubes off your body will be disastrous. That's why they tied your hand and body."

The nurse said, "You have not been a good boy. You were trying to pull them off in your sleep. Perhaps, you didn't even know that. Now that you are awake and if you promise to behave, we can arrange to get you off the artificial breathing."

Beginning Of A Miraculous Recovery

I did not realize what the nurse meant about my artificial breathing, not until I met a couple of professional healthcare personnel who entered my room. I cannot remember what day it was. Was it the same day or the day after? I cannot remember.

However, they said to me that they were going to replace my artificial breathing tube with my own breathing tube. They explained the procedure - how they were going to do that. I did not fully understand.

They continued to explain that, during the emergency last Saturday, the doctors had to pop something out of my throat and replace it with the artificial breathing system. Now the time has come to reverse the situation. I didn't understand what they meant.

I was extremely shocked to know that part of my breathing and/or voice mechanism could be taken out.

"How is that possible? How can that come out of my throat?" I was wondering.

One of the nurses brought my own replaced part in a tray and showed it to me. "Take a look! This is your own," she said. I looked at it and it looked not too tiny. I wondered how did this pop out?

"If you put that in my throat, I'm going to be choked," I wrote on the clip board.

They said, "Don't worry. It came out of there ok, and it should go back there ok. First few minutes you will feel uncomfortable, but after a few minutes longer you will feel much better. There is nothing better than your own breathing mechanism. You will feel much better soon after the replacement."

I wrote, "Where was it kept all this time? Where did you get it from?"

One of the nurses said it was in the fridge all this time.

I watched them how efficiently they replaced the mechanism. It didn't take that long. Initially, my throat felt irritated, but then it calmed down. I was not allowed to talk for some time. Even though I got my own system back, they still kept me on oxygen supply through my nose. By the time, they completed their tasks, I felt exhausted and fell asleep again.

I remember seeing my wife sitting beside me a few times. She told me that she never felt so helpless like this before. My sudden departure from this earth was a total shock to her. It was completely unexpected.

As she was having a light discussion, I remember a couple of doctors who came to visit me that day. One was our family physician, Dr. M. D. He has been a well-respected physician at this hospital. He checked my pulse and looked at the chart.

He said, "Your condition is still very unstable. All of the problems you had earlier are still there. How do you feel now?"

I did not know how to respond to his question. I simply did not know how I felt. The doctor left the room saying that he would be back again.

After the doctor left the room my wife continued to lament, "See, the danger period is not over yet. Anything still could happen to you. You cannot leave us alone. We need you."

Somehow I managed to tell her briefly that I was at the Gateway to the Kingdom of Heaven, and I met God. God said to me, "I am sending you back to the earth."

She said to me, "I will listen to it later. Don't talk too much now. The nurse told you not to get over exhausted."

I remember another doctor who visited me that day. His name was Dr. P. C. He came to check if I was making any progress. He was the designated surgeon, who would be doing the gall bladder surgery, and he would also like to probe if there were any ruptured stones in the vicinity.

He said that he would come to check my status almost daily so that he could assign a date and time for my gall bladder operation.

He also said that several tests would be required prior to his establishing the date and time.

He mentioned several tests, but I remember one of them was a nuclear test that I had to take within the next few days prior to the surgery. After checking my chart, Dr. P. C. left.

I remember Dr. P. V. also visited me that day, keeping an eye on my status.

Soon the night fell, and the visiting hours ended. My wife had left for home. I had slept off and on throughout the night.

The next morning was Wednesday, October 25. A female doctor came in and introduced herself as Dr. E. S. She said that she was in charge of the infectious disease control. She would visit me on a regular basis, and I should not hesitate to contact her anytime, if there was a need.

As usual, Dr. M. D. came to check my status. He said that I would be going through a series of tests for them to find out the exact status of my gall bladder and a few other organs. Dr. M. D. mentioned that, although my condition was slightly better than the previous day, the condition would need to get more stabilized prior to confirming a date for my gall bladder surgery.

Dr. P. C. also came, and he expressed hope that a surgery can be scheduled soon, if the progress continues in the same manner. He said that he would be back again the next day.

I believe it was the same day when I had a number of my colleagues who came to visit me. I remember a few names: Ted Neale, David Stech, Bud Koller, Regis Minerd, Kelly Grudzinski, John Higgs and a few others. They are not only my colleagues, they are my good friends. I am fortunate to have a number of good friends like them. They visited me often while I was in the hospital. They were all genuinely concerned for me, and they stuck with me throughout the entire episode.

I believe it was also the same day when my blood sugar went too low due to improper mixes of the insulin in my intra-venous system. My daughter and my wife were present at the time. I was having a conversation with them. All of a sudden I started to say things such as, "Let's go home! This is not our home! What are we doing here, etc., etc.?"

Soon, I went into a convulsion. Fortunately, the RN was readily available to give me a glucose shot, and quickly thereafter I came to my senses again.

Dr. P. V. also came to visit me before the evening was over. He also said that the situation would need to get further stabilized prior to having a surgery. "You are doing well. Keep it up!" said the doctor to me prior to leaving the room.

The next morning, Thursday, October 26, my wife came early in the morning, as I was scheduled to have a number of tests done.

One of them was a nuclear test. That test did not go well. First of all, there was a delay to start and, when I was taken down there, I had to lie down in a stationary position for more than an hour and a half underneath the special x-ray machine, I was not allowed to move at all. It was very difficult for me to stay in the same position for that length of time.

When the test was over, the technician told me, "You need to come back, and we will need to do it all over again."

I asked him for the reason and he said, "The machine was not working."

I was extremely disappointed and asked him for what purpose I had been lying in the same position for that long and why did they not discontinue the test earlier. I was so disappointed that I said to him, "I do not want to go through the same ordeal again."

They took me back to my room. I was very upset. My wife asked me to calm down. But I remained upset for some time. A few hours later, the technicians called me again for the same test, and I said that I did not want to go through the same ordeal again. It was nothing but a torture, as well as punishment, for me, and it did not show any result.

As usual, Dr. E. S., Dr. M. D. and Dr. P. C. came to see my progress. Both Dr. M. D. and Dr. P. C. indicated that my condition was getting better and if the progress continued, I might be scheduled for my gall bladder surgery for Saturday, October 28.

Both of them asked me to get myself mentally prepared for the operation. Dr. M. D. commented on my progress stating that it was amazing how my condition was improving especially when I was not having any direct medication to remedy the root causes.

Later that day Dr. U. K. also visited me. He looked through all of my charts and reports.

He said to me, "It is a miraculous improvement! You are doing really well. With this kind of progress undoubtedly we can proceed with the gall bladder operation."

He stayed in the room for a few minutes longer, and he told me that he had been associated with this hospital for the past forty-two years. With the complication I had, he found my amazing recovery to be a miraculous situation. He also asked me to keep it up and be mentally prepared for the upcoming surgery.

I was ready to tell Dr. U. K. what actually transpired outside this world as I met God at the Gateway to the Kingdom of Heaven when God said to me, "I am sending you back to the earth. Go back until I see you again next time." But then I thought that it might not be the appropriate moment to disclose this truth to a senior medical professional. Therefore, I remained silent for the time being. My wife thanked Dr. U. K. for his visit, and he said that he would see me again prior to the scheduled date of operation.

When the visiting hours were over that evening my wife and my daughter left for home. I kept thinking, "What actually did take place last Saturday?" I became curious to find out. I decided to ask Dr. M. D., as well as my wife when I see them again next time.

The next morning was Friday, October 27. Dr. E. S. was always the very first doctor who came to see me. As usual, Dr. M. D. also came to see me. I was going to ask him for the details about the previous Saturday, but before I could, he said to me, "Listen! I need to tell you something. I will not be able to come and see you for the next seven days. I'll be away."

I asked him where he was going. He said, "I will be going to San Francisco to attend a medical seminar."

He continued to say, "Don't worry! I arranged for another doctor. His name is Dr. M. L. and he will look after you on my behalf while I am gone."

"Dr. M. L. is a good doctor and I've known him for quite some time. You will be in good hands. Dr. M. L. will also keep me informed of your progress. You be good. I want to see you in good shape after I return," he checked my reports and left.

After Dr. M. D. left, I was a little sad for two reasons: first, I did not expect him to leave until I got better (but then I understood that attending his professional seminars is also important) and second, I did not have a chance to ask him about last Saturday. He seemed to be in a hurry that day. Most likely he had to take care of his last-minute tasks prior to his journey.

I must admit that all of the Registered Nurses and Health Care professionals who took care of me were excellent. They always treated me with utmost care and love. Each person was incredible. I cannot remember all of their names now, but all of them deserve my appreciation, as without their dedication, I could not have gotten better so quickly.

As I was waiting for my wife to arrive that day, the nurse on duty entered the room and monitored the machine. When she finished her task, I asked her, "May I ask you a question?"

She replied, "Certainly."

I said to her, "I really would like to speak to the nurse who attended me last Tuesday when I opened my eyes. Could you kindly find out who that person was and ask her to see me?" She said, "Certainly! I will find out who was on duty that day and let you know." She went away from the room.

A little later, she returned to my room with a young lady. She said to me, "She is the one who was on duty last Tuesday." I looked at her and said, "Sorry! The lady who was here with me was much older." I described how she looked. They said, "Nobody works here by that description." I did not know what to say in response. I stopped asking. But I still remember the face of that motherly-type nurse.

Recollection Of Events

Soon my wife came to see me. After a short conversation, I asked her, "So tell me what exactly happened last Saturday? I would like to know."

She said that after the Emergency Response Team failed to bring me to life in the Intensive Care Unit, some of the doctors decided to send me to the Critical Care Unit so that I could receive a twenty-four hour/around-the-clock care.

I asked, "Why would they send me to the CCU if they could not revive me at ICU?"

She said, "Your breathing stopped and your heart beat stopped. There were no signs of your vital life, but somehow some of the doctors determined that your brain was still functioning. That's the reason they brought you to CCU. They put you on artificial life support immediately. A lot of doctors and nurses had been working on you continuously."

After they moved you to CCU, they stopped everyone from visiting you, including me.

I asked my wife, "What did you do then?"

She said, "Our son, daughter-in-law and our granddaughter, we were asked to wait in the lounge area. We were not allowed to come and see you. I did not know what to do. I was totally at a loss."

She said, "I asked our son to call Frank, Joe and Regis."

Frank is the General Manager of the company I work for. Frank and I have been working for the same company for many years. The relationship is not limited to employer and employee, but also as family and friends. Joe and I have been colleagues for many years. We have been friends for a long period of time. Regis had been my immediate boss for a number of years. Outside of work, our relationship was more like friends, with mutual respect.

She continued, "Frank and his wife, Ann, came very promptly. Soon Regis and his wife, Marilyn, came. Joe came a little later as he had difficulty finding the hospital."

We all sat down and discussed your situation. They were all shocked to hear the update. At one point, Dr. M. D. joined us. He hugged me and said, "His condition is very critical. I am sorry." Dr. M. D. was upset over the whole situation.

She continued, "Dr. U. K. also joined us, and we were all talking about your condition."

She continued, "I said to Dr. M. D., I went to see him, but they would not let me in." They said, 'Only the physicians are allowed.' Dr. M. D. said, "Do you want to see him? Come with me.'"

My wife continued, "I went to see you, along with Dr. M. D. Your condition was very critical. It appeared to me that you had left us forever. I could not stay in that room for long. I came out."

Dr. M. D. said, 'Only one person at a time can go and see him.'

I said, 'Let Frank go first.' Frank came and saw you. He was emotionally distressed after he saw you. Dr. M. D. also allowed our son and daughter-in-law to see you. They all became emotional and did not know what to say. They could not imagine that the situation would turn so critical so suddenly."

I asked, "Do we know what caused me to collapse last Saturday?"

She said, "You remember when the doctor was draining the fluid out of your lung, and I told you I did not see much fluid, but blood. One of your arteries inside the lung got pierced, and it was continuously bleeding inside the lung. Gradually, your lung got filled with blood, your breathing stopped, you collapsed, and your heart stopped. The emergency response team tried their best to revive you, and they were not having much success."

I asked, "What happened after that?"

She continued, "I think the doctors took you to the surgery room. You were there for quite some time. Dr. J. L., who is the top-notch surgeon in this hospital, installed several drain tubes into the left side of your chest and drained the blood out. You were also continuously given blood transfusion, since you had already lost most of your own blood."

She said, "Then it was getting late at night. One by one, they all left, and we also went home."

She continued, "On our journey back home I said to our son and daughter-in-law not to say anything about your collapse and the critical situation to our daughter. Up until then, she was completely in the dark of your situation. She will not be able to handle this news emotionally. I told them, 'We will gradually disclose the situation.'"

They nodded.

I asked her, "Does she know by now what happened to me?"

"Not quite," she said, "She knows only bits and pieces. You are going through a series of tests, and you will be in the hospital for some time."

Soon it was late afternoon of that day. I told my wife to go to the cafeteria downstairs and have something to eat. She was always on the go; she was not taking care of herself; she was not having her meals routinely; she had no time for herself. Reluctantly, she went downstairs to the cafeteria.

Bud Koller, a good friend of mine came to see me. We spoke for a while, and, when my wife returned to the room, Bud stayed for a few minutes longer and then he left. No other doctor visited me that day. I was still waiting for a confirmation as to whether or not I was going to have the surgery the next day.

The next morning, Saturday, October 28, Dr. M. L. came to see me. I asked him if I was going to have the surgery that day. He said that he was not sure, and it was all up to Dr. P. C., the surgeon.

Later, Dr. P. C. came to see me and advised that he decided to postpone my operation until Monday, October 30. He continued, "During the weekend, the doctors usually take care of the emergencies only." He said that it would work better for him, as well as for me, if he scheduled it for Monday. I agreed.

During that weekend, I had a number of visitors - colleagues from my workplace, as well as family and friends. Dr. U. K. also came to see me on both Saturday and Sunday. He stayed for a little longer than normal and tried to cheer me up. He said that my condition was getting stabilized for the operation. He said, "It is better that the operation got postponed until Monday. By Monday, your condition would get a little more stabilized." He also commented that it was a miraculous improvement. He wished me well for my surgery on Monday and left.

Gangrenous Gall Bladder

On Monday, October 30, my wife came to see me early. In the morning, I was going through the pre-surgery procedures. I was not concerned. I knew that God would not have sent me back to the earth with some specific instructions for me to follow if He had to call me back to Him so soon. I knew that I would be fine.

I was mentally prepared for the operation. I think my wife was concerned. Of course, she had all the reasons to be concerned. Considering all the circumstances I was going through since October 18 and the fact that she was with me at each step of the way, that experience alone would be sufficient reason for her to be worried.

She asked me, "You are still weak. What do you think? Will you be ok to go through this? I am worried for you." I said to her, "Don't worry! I'm prepared to go through this. Let's get it done! I will be ok."

Soon they took me to the operating room. Once I was there I was given the anesthesia, and within a few seconds I fell into deep sleep. Later, when I was recovering from the anesthesia, I saw Dr. P. C. was standing beside me and talking to me. He was saying, "Everything went fine. We will keep you for a few minutes longer under observation before we can send you back to your room."

I asked if my wife was anywhere nearby. The doctor said that they would call her, and she would be allowed to come in.

My wife soon came by me. She said, "Thank God! Everything went smoothly."

I asked her how long it took. I believe she said it was about two to three hours since I came in. She held my hand and said, "I was waiting at the lounge. The doctor came to see me after the operation and sat beside me. The doctor said that he removed the gall bladder. He also removed the stones. He took more time than normal as he was carefully probing the surrounding areas. He said that everything went fine. They would also do some biopsy on the removed gall bladder for further analysis."

My wife stayed with me while the nurses were keeping an eye on me every few minutes. They were continuously monitoring my vitals, and, when they were convinced that I was ok to go back to my room, they sent me there.

The nurses on my floor were excited to see me back and were anxious to make me feel comfortable. They quickly transferred me to my bed and adjusted the position. I was still under the influence of anesthesia and my mind was still foggy.

I believe Dr. M. L. came to see me twice that day, once prior to the surgery and again after the surgery. I remember I also had a few floor physicians who came to see me, and they were looking at my charts and checking the results of my operation.

By that evening the test results of my removed gall bladder was in my room. I remember one member of the medical team showing me my gall bladder and some stones that were removed from my body. They were kept inside a plastic or glass container. I was also advised that the removed gall bladder was "gangrenous". My wife asked, "What does that mean?"

The person said, "In plain English, he has been very lucky. If the gall bladder was not removed from his body at this time, the gangrene set in his gall bladder would remove him from this world. Gangrenes are very nasty and deadly."

When the medical person left the room, my wife said, "Thank God! The gangrenous gall bladder was removed right in time. Otherwise, it would have been too late."

Later, when the nurse was changing the dressings from the incision areas, I noticed that a tube was protruding from the right side of my stomach into a bulb-shaped container. I asked the nurse what that was for. She said it was meant for drainage of the excess bile. It had to be frequently monitored. Whenever it was near full, it needed to be drained, measured and recorded each time. She also said, "It will stay there for several days until the surgeon removes it from your body."

In the evening, my daughter came to see me, and my wife returned home with her after the regular visiting hours were over.

I could not sleep that night, since I felt that I was taken over by different kinds of pain. The pain from the wounds of incisions had taken over my whole body. At times, it was intolerable and prevented me from falling asleep. For the first time in my life, I asked the attending RN for some pain killers. I never liked taking any pain killers and always avoided them.

I was then given pain killers, but I noticed the effect was not long lasting and very temporary. At the same time, I was having nightmares or some weird dreams, such as I was forcefully kept in a house. I wanted to escape from there but had no way of getting out, since the people who forcefully kept me there were watching me all the time. As long as the pain killers were in effect, I was not feeling the pain as my mind was occupied with having the same weird dream over and over. It was a very strange feeling, and I never enjoyed these dreams.

The night passed somehow, and then it was Tuesday, October 31. As usual, Dr. E. S. came to see me in the morning. A little later, Dr. M. L. also came. Nothing much happened that day. I was trying to recover from the pains of the surgery.

Mini Surgery & Oxygen Therapy

Later that evening, I noticed that I was experiencing difficulty breathing again. My wife stayed with me practically the whole day and went home after the regular visiting hours were over.

I fell asleep. Sometime late in the night, I was awakened by the resident nurse and the doctor. They were very concerned by an earlier x-ray that showed that I was having some fresh blood in my lungs which was not getting drained out. They said that I needed another drain tube put in my lungs immediately, or things might get complicated.

The resident doctor, the registered nurse and a patient care assistant prepared themselves for a mini-surgery right there in my bed. The doctor applied the local anesthesia and performed the mini-surgery and implanted another drain tube from my left lung. I was not put to sleep. Therefore, I was able to look at the entire operation.

After the medical team left the room, I began to wonder if the operation was carried out properly and whether or not it should have been done in the proper surgery room by a more experienced surgical team. I said to myself, "There must be something wrong inside, and they could not wait that long."

I decided to ask my doctor about this when I saw him the next time. But Dr. M. D., my family physician, still had not returned from his San Francisco trip.

The next day, November 1, when Dr. M. L. came to visit me, I told him what actually happened the night before. I asked him whether the mini-surgery conducted in the room was a routine procedure. I also asked him, "If my condition had gotten worse and if there were complications, how would that be handled?"

Dr. M. L. was surprised to hear that such an operation took place without the consent of the patient or a close family member. He said,

"Normally, the hospital should have contacted your spouse or a nearest family member advising of the situation." He did not know why it was not done.

My wife came to see me later, and I told her about the previous night. She was completely in the dark up to that point not knowing that such an action had taken place, and she was completely unaware of it. She wanted to ask the hospital administrator for an explanation. I told her not to pursue the matter any further, as this could complicate the medical treatment.

She said that a lot of things happened in the last two weeks, and she was not objecting to the unscheduled operation being done in the room. She said, "At least they could have advised me what they were going to do, and I could have been present at the time."

I told her not to worry about it, since everything went fine.

But everything was not fine. My problem with breathing started to get worse. Soon, I was put back on the oxygen tube. Also, I was placed on the breathing therapy several times a day.

Soon the night fell, and visiting hours were over. My wife insisted that she was not going back home. She would rather stay there with me throughout the night. At least she would be able to keep an eye on me. I said to her, "There are nurses and other health care professionals who are here, and it is their job to take care of me. Perhaps, they won't allow you to stay."

She went out and came back a few minutes later. She said, "I asked the RN, and there was no problem for me to stay here overnight."

She pointed to a chair in the room and said, "This chair can fold into a bed, and I can sleep here. They will provide me with the pillows and cover sheets."

Even though I was concerned for the lack of her comfort, I noticed that she was quite pleased with the arrangement, and she looked happy. I was also happy to see her staying in the room, as I could have a companion and someone to talk to during the night should there be a need.

The night progressed. I asked her a few times if she was comfortable lying there, and she said she was fine.

As the night progressed, I was having more difficulty in breathing and I was in terrible discomfort. We take a lot of things for granted when we are healthy - breathing is one of them. It is one of the very basic needs for our survival. I'd have never realized how important breathing was until I was in terrible discomfort.

I was immediately put on oxygen therapy. The RN kept increasing the percentage of oxygen, and, at one point, she raised the percentage of oxygen to 100%. I was always under the impression that 100% oxygen would be the purest and the most desirable form of air that we would like to breathe. When she said that I had to have one hundred percent oxygen therapy for the next four to six hours, I thought, "Great! I am going to have pure oxygen to inhale for that long period of time. It is cool."

But I was totally wrong about my thought. This therapy was so uncomfortable, and it definitely felt like torture. Sometimes, when I could not tolerate it any more, I was disconnecting the attachment from my nose and mouth. The RN was observing me all the time, and every time I was disconnecting it for a few seconds she would get angry at me. She said that if I did it one more time she would put my hands in a restraint.

Occasionally, I could not tolerate it anymore and cried out loudly several times, begging her to stop this therapy. But the therapy did not stop. It continued through the entire night into the next morning.

Now it was Thursday, November 2. The ratio of oxygen was gradually reduced much lower. I said to myself, "What a relief! Finally, the torture has stopped."

Major Lung Surgery

As usual, Dr. E. S. came to see me in the morning. She asked me typically the same questions. Dr. M. L. also came to see me, along with Dr. U. K. The doctors advised that I would have to go through several x-rays that day and the next morning. Depending on the results of the x-rays, a decision would be made as to whether or not I would need a surgery in my lungs. Accordingly, I was scheduled to have several x-rays that day.

When the results of the x-rays were received, I was advised by the resident doctor that a surgery was necessary. I was advised that it would be scheduled for Friday, November 3. I was also advised that this would be considered a major surgery, since it would take many hours in the operating room.

My wife asked the doctor, "Do you think he is medically fit to go through such a long procedure?"

The doctor said. "We have no alternatives. This surgery is absolutely necessary for his well-being. If we do not proceed with this, the consequences will not be good."

The doctor continued, "On the brighter side, let me tell you, you are fortunate that the surgery will be performed by Dr. J. L. who is associated with a world class hospital and considered to be one of the best doctors. He is well regarded as one of the top-notch surgeons."

The doctor continued, "We would put you on pre-surgical procedures tonight, and you would not be allowed to have any food or drinks for x number of hours. In the morning, you will need to have a few more x-rays prior to going to the operating room." The doctor then left the room.

My wife appeared to be nervous. She wanted me to get better, but she was not sure if physically I would be able to withstand such a major operation. She said to me, "You just went through a surgery last Monday. Today is Thursday. Not even four days have gone by. Now, they are talking about another major operation tomorrow that is supposed to last many hours. How would you handle this one? You have not yet recovered from the last one. You are still having aches and pains from the last incisions." I saw her mental stress and agony and realized what she was going through.

I said to my wife, "Don't worry. Everything will be fine. Dr. J. L. is the same doctor who put my drain tubes in the first place. I still have the tubes hanging on the left side of my chest. Dr. J. L. is a good surgeon. He came to see me several times and looks like a very caring type. I have full confidence in him. Nothing will happen to me."

She was still not feeling at ease with the situation. I insisted that she go home that night, since she needed a good night's sleep. The previous night, she was awake the whole night because of my 100% oxygen therapy. She saw throughout the entire night how uncomfortable I felt with that therapy.

I also suggested that she call our son and ask him to be present during the surgery. He lives in the state of Michigan. If he could stay with her throughout the operation and until the result was known, that definitely would provide moral support for her. In the event the situation became a crisis, his presence with his Mother would be very beneficial.

My wife went back home in the evening. She called my son and asked him if it was possible for him to take the time off work and be present at the hospital during the operation. My son said that he would be there. He did not know exactly when, but sometime during the day he would be there.

All along I was being nurtured through the inter-venous system. It was disconnected sometime in the evening, since I was expected to undergo the surgery in the morning. The RN came in quite frequently throughout the night to monitor and record various readings for charts that might be necessary for the surgeon to make his final decision.

I knew it would be a major surgery, but I did not feel nervous. I was rather anxious to have it over and done with. I was probably given a few tranquilizers earlier in the evening since I slept fairly well that night, despite my breathing problems and other pains.

Soon it was Friday, November 3. Dr. E. S. came to see me as usual. The technicians came twice to take x-rays. My wife came early in the morning knowing that I would be taken for the operation sometime in the morning, since she wanted to be there.

Sometime in the mid-morning I was taken to the surgery room. Dr. J. L. explained the procedure to me and introduced me to another surgeon who was going to assist him. I believe his name was Dr. J. S. There were a few other doctors and nurses who were discussing the case among themselves. I could gather from the discussions that I would be put on the artificial life support machine again.

My wife was asked to wait in the lounge, since the doctors may want to consult with her from time to time. She wished me "good luck" and went to the lounge.

I believe it was Dr. J. S. who gave me the anesthetics. Immediately, I fell into deep sleep. I had no idea what happened to me or where I was.

It felt very uncomfortable as I was coming off the anesthesia. A few doctors and nurses were talking to me, but I did not understand what they were saying. It felt strange because I was breathing through the artificial life support again.

It was so uncomfortable, and I was wishing to go back to sleep again. It felt like something strange had been stuck to my throat, and I could not move or get rid of it. I was dozing on and off again. I had absolutely no clue where I was or what I was doing at the time.

I remember seeing my wife once beside me, and then I was sleepy again. I was also feeling very weak. There were two nurses by my side, and they were saying something to me, but I did not understand one word.

I do not know how long I was in the recovery room. I do remember one doctor coming to me and saying, "You have been very brave. Everything is fine." At one point, I was thinking, "Why is it night-time already? I remember I came here in the morning. Why is it so dark already? It feels like it is quite late in the night."

I remember bits and pieces of my recovery. Once when I opened my eyes, I saw I was getting a blood transfusion. Another time I saw my hands and legs were restrained again like the previous time. I remember a doctor or a technician continuously monitoring the artificial breathing machine.

I do not know exactly when I came back to my full senses after the operation. It could very well have been the following morning, Saturday, November 4.

I remember seeing Dr. M. L., who told me that it was a very long operation, and I had lost a lot of blood. Consequently, they had to replenish the blood. He also said that the blood level in my system was still dangerously low, and he was keeping an eye on it. Should the blood level continue to slide, he would put in a request for another transfusion. Dr. M. L. also said that Dr. M. D., my family physician had returned from his trip, and he would visit me soon.

I saw my wife a few times after the operation. However, I was not able to have a direct communication, since I was not steady. When I saw her later, I asked her if she managed to get some sleep the night before, and she said, "I did."

I asked her, "How long was I in the operating room?"

She said, "You were there five to six hours. But, since you had problems coming off the anesthesia, it took much longer."

I asked her, "What did you do all this time? Didn't you get bored?"

She said, "I was waiting in the lounge area. At one point, Dr. P. V. saw me and sat beside me. We discussed your operation, and he gave me moral support."

"What about our son? Did he ever come and stay with you, and how long did he stay?" I asked.

She said, "He came late and stayed for a while. He was continuously on his cell phone, and he had to leave early because he had some urgent business to take care of."

I asked, "Did he call you after he left?" She said, "Yes, and said he would be back on Sunday."

She continued, "I was waiting in the lounge for a long period of time. It felt like time was at a standstill. I could not go anywhere, since I was afraid that, if I went somewhere, Dr. J. L. might come out and look for me. He would probably go back to the operating room without talking to me. I was getting tensed as hours went by, and the doctor did not come out of the operating room. I was wondering if everything was going alright in the surgery area."

"Then, finally, the doctor came out, shook my hand and sat beside me. He said that it was a very complex operation. He said that he took extra caution and made sure everything was done properly. He also said that he found some blood stains inside the lungs, and he ensured the stains were all removed. He said that, "If the stains did not get removed, your husband would not be well for long. That is why it took such a long time.""

He paused for a moment and continued, "Let us hope for the best. Your husband will most likely need extra care for some time, even after he recovers from all this."

He again paused for a moment and continued, "You can see him when he is in the recovery room. It will take a while before he recovers completely. He will be on the respiratory machine for some time and will also be receiving blood, since he lost some of his own."

My wife said, "Thank you, Dr. L.! Thank you so much for your extra care and dedication. We really appreciate it."

The doctor said, "You are welcome! You may come with me if you wish to peek at him. He must be in the recovery room."

My wife followed.

"What happened after that?" I asked.

She said, "You were still in a deep sleep and breathing through the respiratory machine again like last time. A couple of nurses were observing you. They said, "It may take another half an hour to an hour. You may go some place and come back again.""

My wife said, "I went to the cafeteria downstairs, had a cup of tea and light snack. I returned to the recovery room, and you were still not awake. The nurses said, "He is taking his time. You may go out for another round and come back.""

"Gradually, all of the other patients who had surgeries earlier recovered and returned to their rooms. You were the only one remaining there. A few nurses and a small medical team were waiting for you to wake up so they could send you back to your room before they could call it a day."

"When you were finally brought to your room, a medical team was continuously working with the breathing machine for a long period of time. Your hands and feet were restrained one more time. The medical team said that they would remain with you until the respiratory machine was replaced by a normal oxygen tube."

My wife said, "I returned home after the normal visiting hours were over, since you needed a complete rest from the long surgery."

Amazing Bounce Back To Life

The next day, Saturday, November 4, Dr. M. D., my family physician came to see me, and I was delighted to see him back. The last time I saw him was a week earlier on Friday, October 27.

I suppose that Dr. M. D. was also anxious to see me, since he said that he came straight from the airport. He was on his way home and decided to stop by and see how I was doing.

He asked me how I was feeling. I said, "Much better than last time when you saw me."

He looked at my charts and said, "It is a miracle. I'm really impressed. Your condition is much better. If you keep it up, you will be able to go home soon."

This is the first time I heard any doctor speaking to me about the possibility of going home. I can now feel the joy of hope. Just a mere thought of going home cheered me up. Was I really seeing the light at the end of tunnel? I asked myself.

Dr. M. D. left the room to speak to the resident staff and came back a few minutes later.

"Just hang in there, and I will see you tomorrow. Keep it up. You are doing great," he said to me before he left.

I asked my wife if she wanted to go home and take some rest. She said, "I can take some rest here on this chair." I agreed.

As far as I can recall, she had stayed in the room for several nights. She always kept an eye on me and made sure that I was not feeling depressed. Sometimes I was getting concerned for her not getting enough sleep, but she was happy to be there with me.

The night passed, and then it was Sunday, November 5. Both Dr. M. D. and Dr. M. L. came to see me and they were pleased with the progress I was making.

Shortly before noon my son, my daughter-in-law and my granddaughter came to see me. My wife and I were both very happy to see them. I told them that their mother needed to get out of this room. I told them that I was doing much better, and it was time to celebrate. I asked them to go to a good restaurant and enjoy a good lunch. They complied.

After a few hours, they came back. We chatted for a while, and they departed shortly thereafter. My wife left with them also, since they indicated they would drop her home.

After they left, later that evening, my blood sugar dropped too low again due to a high amount of insulin in the system. It dropped so low that I went into a convulsion, and luckily there was a doctor nearby. The nurse told me the next day that the doctor gave me a glucose shot, and soon I was back to my senses.

When my wife found out about the incident the next day (Monday, November 6), that I was on convulsion again for the second time, she was not too pleased. She said to me, "For the next few days, until you get released from this hospital, I am staying here in this room day and night. I cannot afford to lose you again." I said to her, "Nobody did it on purpose. Mistakes do happen. That's why we are humans."

"They should be more careful, as it is a matter of life and death," she said. Later, when the nurse came to my room, the nurse apologized to me for what happened the previous night. She said that it was an honest mistake, and she felt very sorry for the incident. My wife calmed down, and we all were friends again.

A number of doctors visited me on Monday, November 6. They were Dr. E. S., Dr. G. H., Dr. J. S., Dr. M. D., Dr. P. V., Dr. J. L., and Dr. R. F.

Everyone congratulated me on my impressive recovery. A few of them commented to me that it was undoubtedly a miraculous, hard to believe type of recovery.

Dr. J. L. said to me, "As soon as the drain pipes come off your chest, you would be able to go home."

I asked Dr. J. L., "When do you think they will come off?" He said, "Within a few days. I have to ask them to take x-rays of your chest daily. I will take them off as soon as the x-rays indicate that they could come off."

Dr. J. L. also suggested for me to start walking a couple of times each day. "You will need to gain your strength back before we can release you from the hospital."

Dr. R. F. came to me and said, "Good Luck and Best Wishes to you. You do not need me anymore. Therefore, I will not see you again."

He said to me that he enjoyed working with my case. He wished me well and shook my hands before he left. Both my wife and I thanked him for his dedication and care.

Unexpected Apology From Dr. X

Around the same time, both my wife and I noticed that Dr. X, who did the surgery at my back on Saturday, October 21, had been coming by my room quite frequently as if he wanted to say something to me.

Every time he came by my room, both my wife and I were not happy to see him at all. As a matter of fact, whenever he came by us, we were feeling tensed up. When my family physician, Dr. M. D. came to see me, we requested him to tell Dr. X that he needs to stay away from this room. We really did not want to see him again.

However, one day shortly thereafter, Dr. X came to my room, and my wife was there in the room at that time.

He told me, "Listen, I know you do not want to see me, and I do not blame you for that. But I have to say something to you. Please grant me a couple of minutes. I know you get disturbed to see me. Please let me say what I need to say, and then I will not disturb you again."

I looked at my wife, and she looked at me. I said, "Ok, go ahead, you may continue."

The doctor said, "I have been trying to come and speak to you several times in the past few weeks. All my attempts have failed thus far. Every time I came to speak to you either you had someone in the room or you were not in a position to talk. I know you have told your doctor that you do not wish to see me near your room. But I need to tell you something so that I can get it off my chest."

I asked, "What do you want tell me?"

The doctor said, "I have come to ask for your forgiveness. Because of me, you have suffered a lot. I am so sorry. I have caused you a great deal of suffering and pain. Please forgive me. Unless you forgive me, I will not be able to rest in peace."

My wife and I looked at each other. While we were trying to decide how to respond to this unexpected situation, the doctor continued to say, "I have been practicing here for the past twelve or thirteen years. Anything like this has never happened before."

I remained quiet for a moment. The doctor continued, "Ever since that day I was not able to sleep at night. It keeps bothering me, and I cannot forgive myself. I stay awake most of the time at night, looking at the ceiling of my bedroom."

He continued to say, "I guess it proves that we are all human beings. Just because we are doctors does not mean that we do not make mistakes. I just want you to know that I did not do it on purpose. It was not intentional. I just feel so sorry, and I apologize to you. Please forgive me if you can."

I looked at my wife to watch her reaction whether or not I should accept his apology. She nodded.

I said to the doctor, "Doctor X, you have realized that you have made a mistake, and you said that you have not done this intentionally. Even though you are a doctor, you are still a human being, and all humans make mistakes. I am not keeping any grudges against you. You can rest in peace."

The doctor was touched by my comments. He shook my hand, and wished me well and a speedy recovery. He also thanked us for our forgiveness and said that he felt much lighter, as if a big burden had been removed from his chest.

After the doctor left the room, I started to think, "This doctor is obviously very much disturbed by the circumstances that caused the situation to go totally out of control, and his conscience must be bothering him so much that he had been persistently trying to speak to me for several days."

However, I started to wonder, "Was the crisis really caused by this doctor? Or was there an Invisible Force Who had been working mysteriously behind the scenes to draw our attention?"

There is no doubt in my mind that an Invisible Force was entirely responsible for the episode. I am thoroughly convinced that The Invisible Force was orchestrating the whole thing. What would be the purpose? That is still a mystery and far beyond our comprehension. How can we understand what goes through the logic of Infinity with our finite mind? We simply cannot.

Conversation With God

Let me go back to the Gateway of the Kingdom of Heaven and refresh how I met God and how the conversations went.

Back on the altar at the Gateway, as I was looking towards the center of the high walled platform, my eyes were struck in awe at what I saw. At the center of that location was a huge throne. Lo and behold! There was the Lord! The Lord was sitting on the throne!

As soon as I saw Him, I knew He was the Supreme Lord! I started to tremble with fear! He was so huge. Here, I am 5'6" tall, standing at the extreme far left corner and looking at the center of that altar, and He is approximately 600 feet away from me. He was sitting on the throne, and, at that sitting position, He appeared to be approximately 35 to 40 feet tall. Therefore, when He stands up, I presume He would be about 70 feet tall. He was very well proportioned and wore a white robe.

I again started to tremble with fear, and my knees felt very weak. I was standing at the extreme far edge of the platform, and I could very easily fall off the edge with my fearful trembling. He was such a powerful, overwhelming and mesmerizing figure that I could not look at Him for too long. I was trembling with fear so much thinking that this would be the end of my life. The Lord will not spare me.

I looked slightly towards the left of the throne (right from my position) and was amazed to see a very Narrow Door. The door was so narrow that it struck me as completely out of proportion. I now realized that this Narrow Door is the only entrance to the inside of the Kingdom of Heaven. This is the only entrance in the entire perimeter of the compound. This is the entrance for which I had been searching.

"How do I go through this door?" I asked myself. The Lord is so big and frightening I cannot dare myself to go near the door. It was quite evident to me that I could not even try to enter through the door, unless the Lord allowed me to go through the door.

It had been also pretty clear to me that I was now standing at the Gateway to the Kingdom of Heaven, and I was completely at the mercy of the Lord. I was still nervous and shaky, but then the Lord spoke to me.

He had a very deep, commanding voice, but, at the same time, I noticed His voice was also a loving one. Language did not seem to be a barrier at all. When the Lord spoke, I could understand that in any of the languages I know. By the same token, it didn't matter in what language I responded - the Lord understood every word, even before I spoke.

The Lord looked at me and asked, "What are you doing here?"

I shrugged my shoulders, meaning, "I do not know."

He said to me in an authoritative, but loving voice, "Your time has not come yet. I'm sending you back to the earth. Go back until your time comes."

By then, I gathered some courage, as I noticed I was not shaking any longer with fear. The Lord continued, "Go back and complete your unfinished tasks. Love your family. Love your children. Pay attention to your daughter – she needs your help."

Hearing the loving and caring voice of the Lord, I gathered a little more courage, and I asked, "Lord! I'm not worthy of standing before You. I'm a sinner! I have sinned, Lord. How can I be sure that I can enter through this Door next time? Lord, please tell me - when is my next time?"

The Lord did not respond.

I continued to plead, "Lord! Please provide me with some guidance. How can I prepare myself for the next time? How can I make myself worthy of standing before you next time? I do not know how much time I'll have before the next time."

The Lord still did not respond.

I continued pleading, "Please Lord! Please guide me to prepare myself for next time. Please tell me if I need to join any church, any temple, any synagogue, any religious institute, any religious association or any other place. I'll do whatever You say, but please guide me."

The Lord looked at me and said, "No, it is not necessary for you to join any church, any temple or anything else. Those things are not important to Me."

(Although the Lord indicated to me that membership to any religious group is not necessary to enter the Kingdom of Heaven, we, as humans, definitely need a support group to help us through our difficult times, remind us of the importance of worshiping God, teach us in the Ways of the Lord, and assist us in accomplishing His directives.)

The Lord continued, "What is important to Me is your personal relationship with Me, how sincere, how honest, how true are you with Me? That's the only thing that counts."

I looked at the Lord and begged Him to be merciful to me.

I said, "Lord! I am a human being. When I go back, I'll be involved with my day-to-day activities, and I'll be back to my worldly life. Please give me some specific instructions or guidelines that I can follow." I continued to beg for His mercy.

SPECIFIC INSTRUCTIONS FROM GOD

The Lord looked at me and said, "Here are some instructions for you that I want you to follow between now and your next time."

He gave me the following five instructions.

1. "TELL THE TRUTH"

"Go back and tell the Truth. Do not be afraid to tell the Truth. Some people may ridicule upon you when they hear the Truth, but do not despair, be brave and always tell the Truth."

('Truth' here for me has dual meanings. Tell the truth in the sense has meaning 'do not lie'. But, in the broader sense, He is asking me to tell about my experience at the Gateway to the Kingdom of Heaven, my meeting Him in person, my discovery of the one and only Narrow Entry Door to Heaven, His kind conversations with me, His specific instructions to me, and so on. By His first instruction to me He is not only asking me not to lie, but also He is asking me to go back and share my experience with everyone without any fear.)

2. "COMMIT NO MORE SINS"

"From this day on forward, do not commit any more sins. Remember the consequences. The wages of sin is death."

(All my sins up to that day had been forgiven by Him as He is asking me "From this day on forward do not commit any more sins." However, "sin" in the eyes of God may not exactly be the same as we humans view it. We are all committing sins every day knowingly or unknowingly. I try my best not to commit any more sins every day. But our day-to-day life style in this world is such that I cannot say for sure that I am not committing any more sins. What I view as not sin may very well be sinful in the eyes of God. I'll explain a little later in the book how we can be saved from the wages of sin, by genuinely repenting to Him.)

3. "SURRENDER YOURSELF COMPLETELY TO ME IN YOUR DAILY LIFE"

(By this instruction, He is asking me to surrender myself completely to Him. He is asking me to let Him be in the driver's seat. He is asking me to let Him take control over everything that is necessary for me to live through this life. Surrendering myself completely to Him means that He is taking charge of my life, and He will see that all my needs are fulfilled, since He knows what my needs are.)

4. "WALK WITH ME"

(I should have asked God what He specifically meant for me by this instruction. I am still not sure how I can walk with God. I am a human being. How can a human being walk with God? I have asked some of my friends and some spiritual leaders for their interpretations of this instruction. They have been kind enough to provide me with their best explanations, i.e., perhaps it means do not go ahead of me nor fall behind me; hold my hand and walk "with" me. But I am still searching for the true meaning of this instruction. I am hoping that through my prayers and meditation of the Scriptures God will offer His guidance.)

5. "TAKE CARE OF THE POOR"

"Take care of the poor. Open your hearts. Be generous to the poor. They need your help."

Then, He repeated for the second time,

"TAKE CARE OF THE POOR. OPEN YOUR HEARTS. BE GENEROUS TO THEM. THEY NEED YOUR HELP. THIS IS VERY IMPORTANT."

(The word 'Poor' does not mean someone who needs financial help only; it can also mean someone who is physically, mentally, intellectually or spiritually poor and needing help.)

When the Lord repeated for the second time asking me to take care of the poor, stressing that this is very important and I need to be generous to the poor as they need my help and this is a very important instruction.

I said very humbly to the Lord, "Lord! Certainly I will help the poor as much as I can. You know the needs for the poor in the world are far greater than what a small person like me can do. The needs are not only where I live; the needs are everywhere, all over the world."

"Lord! Please forgive me saying this. I will take care of the poor as much as I can, but my efforts will be like a tiny drop of water in the entire ocean. It is not going to make much of an impact."

As I said this to God, I was feeling extremely concerned that I should not have said anything like this to God. Definitely, He will be angry at me, and He will be very annoyed with me. I have no right to speak to Him like this. Who am I to tell God? He knows how big the needs are.

It is with great fear and great respect I said to the Lord, "Lord! Please forgive me for my sins. I should not have said anything like this to You. You are Almighty. You know everything. I did not mean to question your instruction. I am a simple human being. I am only trying to state that the needs to help the poor are far greater than what a small person like me can accomplish. Please forgive me. I beg for Your mercy!"

I was waiting for God to get angry at me and punish me for my rudeness. However, I was pleasantly surprised as I noticed that He was not annoyed with me at all. Instead, with a deep loving voice, He said to me, "Listen carefully! I am assigning you with a few tasks when you are back on the earth. I want you to complete your unfinished tasks. When you are back to the earth I want you to write two books."

He continued, "Go back and write the first book about telling the Truth; about your experience; and about this conversation as it is taking place between you and Me. Do not be afraid to be truthful. I will ensure that this book reaches to the readers everywhere in the world."

The Lord looked at me and said, "For these tasks I am also giving you two guidelines for you to follow. You must remember them always. They are important."

"First, each and every penny that you will receive from the sales of the two books, you must give them away to the cause of the poor. You must not keep one penny from the proceeds for yourself. This is very important!"

"Second, you need to let your readers know that it is not important to Me at all whatever church, temple or religious institution they belong to. The most important one to Me is each person's own personal relationship with Me. I am only interested to know how sincere, how honest, how true they are with Me. Tell your readers that the five instructions that I am asking you to obey between now and your next time, the same instructions equally apply for every mankind. The fifth instruction is particularly important to each and every person. Everyone needs to open their hearts and be generous to the poor. I expect it from everyone."

I said to the Lord, "Thank You, Lord! Thank You for Your mercy! Lord, forgive me, I have never written a book in my life. But I will write as You are assigning the tasks to me. Please give me the strength and the courage so that I can complete my assignments. Lord, you said for me to write two books. When do you want me to write the second book?"

The Lord said, "Write the first one soon after you are back on your feet and then wait for a year or two before you start the next one. Do not be afraid. I will be with you and I will guide you."

By then, I noticed that I was not feeling afraid of God any more. To me, He was very kind, loving, and like a true friend with genuine concern for each and every one of us.

I asked God a few more questions. He answered all of them. It will not be appropriate for me to share the rest of the conversations with all my readers, since they are a bit personal and related to my family members. I sincerely apologize to my readers for not disclosing them.

When we finished our conversation, God said to me, "I am now sending you back to the earth. Go back and complete your unfinished tasks. When the time comes I will see you again."

I thanked the Lord for His Mercy and Love to me.

Next thing I remember is opening my eyes and seeing a loving, motherly type nurse looking at me in the hospital room. Who was that nurse?

I remember very clearly about my journey from the earth to the Gateway of the Kingdom of Heaven. I described that journey earlier in this book. I was following a very bright light at a tremendous speed for a considerable amount of time until I reached my destination on the other side.

But I do not remember anything at all how I returned from the Gateway to the Kingdom of Heaven back to the earth. However, I know one thing for sure - this is a journey that I was not allowed to do on my own. A companion bright Light had to take me there.

The question still remains - how did I get back from there to here? Considering this is a journey I cannot make on my own, someone had to bring me back from there to here.

Was the loving motherly type nurse whom I saw was none other than an Angel sent by God? Was it her assignment to return me to my destination back to the earth, safe and sound?

This will remain a mystery to me for the rest of my life.

Release From The Hospital

Meanwhile, back in the hospital, my progress was remarkably fast. All of the drain tubes came off my chest one by one. My IV tubes came off. For the first time in three weeks I was allowed to have solid food, namely, Jell-O. All of the tubes that were attached to my body came off one by one. I felt a great relief.

I was bed-ridden all this time. I started to walk again just like a child - first with the help of a trained nurse, then with my wife assisting me, a few times with my visiting friend, Bud, and another few times with an extraordinary Patient Care Assistant named Dan. Dan helped me very often whenever he was on duty.

I remember when Dan took me one afternoon for a short walk outside the door to fetch some fresh air for the first time since I got admitted into the hospital, he said to me, "Can you smell the Pine trees? Try to smell and take a deep breath of fresh air and hold it for a few seconds. Thank the Lord as you are holding it, because we take a lot of things for granted in our life. We do not appreciate the things until they are taken away from us."

Dan, I will never forget those words as long as I live. You are absolutely right. We do not know how to thank God for all the little things that He gave us to enjoy, such as the smell of a Pine tree and the natural air we breathe for us to survive in our daily life, we definitely take them for granted.

We do not appreciate the Love and Mercy of God for all the little things, not until they are taken away from us. It is absolutely true.

Finally, the day came. It was the day I was anxiously waiting for. Many times I seriously thought that I would never see this day again in my life.

It was Friday, November 10, 2006.

Dr. M. D., my family physician came to my room and announced that I would be released from the hospital that afternoon. However, he said that I would be put under a very close observation. A visiting Home Healthcare Nurse would visit me on a regular basis to observe and monitor my progress.

I was also scheduled to have follow-up visits to most of the doctors and surgeons who took care of me.

My wife accompanied me to all of those visits. Once she asked the doctor, "How can we be certain that his wounded pancreas is completely healed? As far as we know, he did not receive any medications or treatments for it. How do we know that it won't resurface?"

The doctor said, "All the symptoms indicate that he does not currently have any major problem. But to ensure, I'm going to ask for an MRCP."

I asked the doctor, "What is an MRCP?"

The doctor said, "It is sort of an ultrasonic test called Magnetic Resonance Cholangiopancreatography. We will make an appointment for you. It needs to be done in the hospital lab. It is recommended that you fast for two to four hours before the test, and it will take approximately 30 minutes to complete the procedure."

Fearfully I asked, "Do I need to have anesthetics again?"

The doctor replied with a smile, "Not at all. It is a special kind of an x-ray. There is nothing to worry about."

Return To Regular Activities

Within a few weeks of my release from the hospital I completed all of my post-surgery check-ups and required tests. Everything was fine. Dr. M. D. initially released me for half-day at work for a couple of weeks and finally released me for full-day at work. Through the grace of God, I was back to my day-to-day activities in a short period of time.

From the time the trauma started up until the time I met God in person, everything was working against me. My condition at the ICU was getting more and more complicated with one thing after another going for me in the wrong direction. There was no medication; no treatment, not until my heart rate would come down; there was no help in sight. I felt all along that an Invisible Force was working behind the scenes to make His points known to me.

As soon as I met God and when He said to me, "I am sending you back to the earth until I see you again next time," I noticed my conditions started to turn positive with or without explanations.

God provided me with highly skilled surgeons and highly knowledgeable medical teams, in a highly caring environment. Without His help, how could I turn around from the extremely dangerous heart rate condition to go through an extended gall bladder operation within a few days? How was it possible that the gangrenous gall bladder was removed just in time? How was it possible that the gangrenes did not remove me from this world before they were removed? How did I get better from the viral pneumonia? How could I go through a major lung operation and bounce back to normalcy in a couple of days? Most importantly, how did my ruptured pancreas get healed without any medication or treatment?

Miraculous, eh? Any doubts? Trust in God and accept the fact that Miracles still do happen, even today and can happen to any one of us.

The truth is, "Everything is possible when God is on our side. He is a true, loving God."

Trust me when I say to you, "God wants each and every one of us by Him. That is where we belong permanently. Everything else that we seek in this world is temporary."

Inspiration

In conclusion, may I request each and every one of my readers to ask yourself personally, on your own, without the influence of external distractions, being true to your hearts, and knowing that everything is possible, if God is on our side – please ask for yourself, "Am I on God's side? Am I really sincere, true and honest to Him?"

If the answer is 'yes' my dear reader, you have nothing to worry about. The One and Only God Whom I met in heaven is very kind, very loving and a genuine friend. If you are on His side, be rest assured that He will take care of all your needs.

If the answer is 'no' my dear reader, we still can reach God. He wants each and every one of us to be "on His side" because He still loves us, even if we choose to hate Him. He wants us to become one of His loved ones.

How can we do that? We can come very close to God by simply obeying His instructions. I'll elaborate in details on my findings over the next several chapters. Please continue reading.

Before I conclude this chapter, I would like to share one other personal piece of information with my readers. My family physician, Dr. M. D., once asked me in one of my regular visits, "Tell me something. When you were in the hospital, what did you experience? Did you have any after life experiences?"

Initially I thought it was kind of an odd question coming from a reputable physician. Should I say or not? I noticed his question was genuine. I paused for a while and said, "Yes."

He asked, "Do you mind telling me about it? I am very interested to know."

I explained briefly to him how I traveled to an unknown destination with my companion Light; how magnificent was the Kingdom of Heaven;

how I discovered the one and only Narrow Entry Door into Heaven; how and where I met God; His specific instructions to me; etc. etc.

Dr. M. D. said to me that he believed everything I described, because he knew how terrible my condition was and how remarkably I bounced back. "It was amazing!"

I consider myself very fortunate that I was able to see the most beautiful Kingdom of Heaven with my own eyes. I consider myself even more fortunate as I was able to meet God in person and have a Heart-to-heart conversation with Him. He sent me back to the earth, and someday, when I complete my unfinished tasks that He assigned to me, I will see Him again.

However, there will be one difference in me between last time and my next time. Last time, I was really afraid to die like any one of us. Next time, I am not afraid of death any more. As a matter of fact, I am looking forward to that day when I will see Him again.

May God bless you, my dear reader! Please remember the most important instruction. "Take care of the poor. Open your hearts. Be generous to them. They need your help." In whatever way you can, however you can, please help the needy. In return, God will definitely bestow His blessings many folds on you.

Author's Note

After the publication of the first book it was apparent that the book had been touching many lives throughout various corners of the world. I have received numerous comments or feedbacks from many Readers over the years. I still receive a few comments from time to time. I'm thankful to each and every person who wrote to me. Almost all of the comments came via e-mails. Thank you for your honest feedback!

For the second edition of the first book, I added some Readers' Testimonials. I'm leaving them as part of this book so that the Readers can review them. Please note that additional comments and feedbacks received since the publication of the second edition are not included in this Testimonial chapter. I sincerely apologize for that.

But, what I want to say that this is where my Miraculous True Story should have ended. But, it didn't. My Encounter with Him as well as the writing of the two books transformed me totally to a new person. I'm not the same person as I used to be. This new book is a summary of all the changes that transpired with me over the last ten years of my life.

I welcome your honest feedbacks after you read this new book. My e-mail address is sjs2004@att.net

Testimonials received between 2008 and 2010 are included here. Testimonials received after 2010 are not included here as I lost them due to malfunctioning of my computer. My sincere apologies to everyone who wrote to me after 2010, I hope you will forgive me.

Readers' Testimonials about Code Blue 99

I am David's mother. David gave me a copy of your book. I was so impressed, I ordered 12 copies to share with my family and friends. I've always been skeptical when reading about these experiences, but your book has really reached out to me. M.S., Broadview Heights, Ohio

*****

It is the most awesome and interesting book I've ever read! I must also tell you that I cried several times while reading it, and I couldn't wait to meet you. I'm telling all my friends about it, hoping they too will read it. M.R. age 12, Brunswick, Ohio

*****

Insightful - An excellent true short story describing in great detail what awaits us after life on earth. A wonderful read for people of all religions or non-believers. G.C., Bath, Ohio

*****

Fabulous - What a wonderful book! It certainly will inspire you and give you hope for your "future." Read it - you won't regret it – guaranteed. M.N., Broadview Heights, Ohio

*****

Inspirational - This book, Code Blue 99-A Miraculous True Story, is indeed just that, and promises to bring any reader closer to God, as well as provide us with some food for thought regarding what is important while we are living. The author was, in my opinion, chosen by God, to bring this important message to all of us. A wonderful story! Thank you, Sandy Acharjee. E.N., Broadview Heights, Ohio

*****

Humbling and Awe-inspiring Book - Engrossing and awe-inspiring narrative of one person's visit with God. Described in such great detail, and with such conviction, there is little doubt that what he saw and heard is true. It confirms what has been learned in church and is humbling in how little we really know. Mr. Acharjee says he is not a writer, but his writing makes it feel as if he and the reader are sitting together, one-on-one, talking. The story is so engrossing that, once started, it would be very difficult to put it aside. Would be an excellent book for a teenager to read, as well as seniors. It will definitely make the reader pause, think, and, hopefully, act. T.A., Strongsville, Ohio

*****

I have just read your book today, and wanted to let you know how deeply moved I was by it. I first learned of your book on Easter Sunday, as I talked with my brother. My family is facing a difficult time as my elderly mother-in-law suffers from serious illnesses. Your book offered much inspiration. My son, who is only 10, began reading your book yesterday. He is very intrigued by the thoughts you have shared.

I have read/heard of other people that have been clinically dead for a while, later resuscitated in a hospital, and lived to tell about the Light they say they personally experienced. I must admit that in the past, I have viewed such accounts with some skepticism. I don't doubt the sincerity of the authors; but I wondered if they were only dreaming of a Light and Divine Presence as they were physically on the brink between life and death. Yet I've always hoped that God truly exists. After reading your book, I no longer have doubts. Thank you for writing it. M.B., Independence, Ohio

*****

Just finished your book. It was wonderful. Thank you very much. Your faith and conviction in God showed on every page. Because of your book, I feel it's time to know God more. I know He loves me. L.S., Cleveland, Ohio

*****

WOW, I just read your book and your story is truly amazing. I felt many emotions while reading your story and the messages brought back with you; it has really opened my eyes to many things. I have always been a true believer, and I can't wait to share the story with everyone in my life. You are a great man; I have always had the utmost respect for you; I'm sad to hear the details about the pain you and your family experienced throughout the whole ordeal. I am grateful that you are now healthy and that you have such a great story to share about your experiences. God has truly blessed you. G.S., Brecksville, Ohio

*****

Thank you for sending me a copy of your book. As soon as I received the book its cover page impressed me instantly. I read the whole book in one sitting. I must tell you it is a very well written book. The details have touched me. I'm sending you herewith a check for $100. Please donate the additional amount to the needy. It is for a good cause. I wish I could do more. If possible, please send me two more books that I'd like to give them to my family members, one in India and one in France. You are truly a blessed person! T. M., Brantford, Canada

*****

I have read your book while I was traveling by train from Kolkata to Puri. I was extremely amazed to read the contents. I liked the book so much that I'm reading it for the second time. The book is very interesting. If you come to India I want to ask you a few questions in person. It seems to me that you did not write this book for yourself. You wrote it for all of us. Thank you for writing the book. S. A., Kolkata, India

*****

I read your book and I'm absolutely stunned. My elderly father has read the book and he was also stunned. My daughter is currently reading the book and after that my wife wants to read the book. My sister who lives in a distant place wants me to send the book to her. It is absolutely an amazing book and I am telling all my friends to get a copy of the book. Our family is anxiously waiting to meet you in person and hear your experience again from you when you come to India. Please plan to visit us soon. H. G., New Delhi, India

*****

I found the book very interesting. Your donating the money to the needy is very noble. Best wishes. C. M., Brecksville, Ohio

*****

I enjoyed reading your book. I discussed the contents with one of the clergies in our church. You mentioned in the book about the platform or an altar. He said that only the blessed ones are allowed to stand on that platform or altar. You truly are a blessed person. I hope, I too am allowed to stand on that platform when my time comes. I wish your book to be a best seller. D. H., Brecksville, Ohio

*****

I work at an off-shore oil rigging platform in Nigeria with many skilled people primarily from European countries. I was so fascinated after reading your book that I took it to work and shared with many of my colleagues. Someday, I'd like to meet you in person and discuss your experience. R. M., Nigeria, Africa.

*****

All I've heard so far is that you had a near death experience and had a divine encounter of some sort, a visit to heaven where you met God. I am doing some research on this subject at the moment and I am wanting to understand the distinction or difference between the Father, Son and Spirit as God was revealed to you in your experience. Was it as the classical trinity? Can you give me some explanations on this from what you witnessed or as it was shared. What I am wanting to know is - Is Jesus God or just the Son of God, if so how can Jesus be the Son of God and God at the same time. Also if Jesus is God does this mean Almighty God or is that the Father only, and where does the Holy Spirit come in? I know of the scriptures in regards to this but I wondered whether your NDE revealed some insight into this. S.C, Perth, Australia

*****

I read your book this weekend, thoroughly enjoyed, and am again so delighted to have met you in person to be a witness to your miracle. Your book was wonderful…I couldn't put it down and plan to pass on to others… of course I will need to buy more copies. I believe you are a messenger inspired by God. I also know that God has very specific plans for me…and yet I haven't completely figured out what that plan is…other than being a nurse, and being present to give to the poor (mostly emotionally, spiritually, and psychologically as you referred to). I have struggled somewhat with my faith since my son died. D.M., Brecksville, Ohio

*****

The experience that you shared is a miracle, as you have said. It is most evident in the change that has occurred in you, and this cannot happen unless we are transformed by the Lord and surrender to Him. While you were telling me your story, I was marveling, because it was as if you were quoting phrases out of the Holy Bible, which is my frame of reference for faith in God. I have intently studied the writings of the Prophets and Apostles for many years. But yet, if I am correct, you were raised a Hindu and not very familiar with Judaism, Christianity or any such similar writings. This was enlightening to me because you saw what I have read about…G. R., Cleveland, Ohio

*****

I finally just had an opportunity to read the book I purchased from you in October. Don and I are on our way to Florida, and I brought it along, hoping to get a chance to read it. And, I did – out loud, so we were both able to "hear" it. I just had to call you immediately to tell you what a wonderful and moving book it is. My father-in-law is in the hospital with congestive heart failure, and we're going to be seeing him very soon. I am definitely going to tell all our family members and friends about this marvelous book, so they can see for themselves how great it is. Thank you so much for it. J. B., Strongsville, OH

*****

I just finished your book yesterday. It's quite interesting. Overall your book is very impressive. Once it's started to read so it encouraged the readers have to finish the book entirely. After reading this book, I understood that there is someone who control and dictate the entire creatures in a systematic manner. None is super and beyond from HIM. We have to follow HIS commandments all the times. Very few people are lucky like you. The Supreme Power has chosen you to do some important assignment on this planet. Hope you will finish all your remaining work in your new life. If you need any kind of assistance from me to finish your remaining task, please feel free to contact the undersigned. I will do my best that I can.................... God's blessings are always with you to finish your remaining project in your new birth. You will be successful to finish your life mission in this birth under HIS COMMANDMENTS.................. R.G., Rexdale, Canada

*****

I found your book so interesting that I read it three times. I found it very inspiring. I still have a few questions that I'd like to ask you in person. Please let me know when you visit Kolkata next time. A. S., Kolkata, India

*****

Such an honor to have met God. In a way, how lucky and proud you must be. You reached out to hundreds or thousands of people like myself to tell your story. How blessed we are to have the computer to communicate with.

I gave your story to a friend of mine who happens to also be fascinated with near death experiences. He probably will tell someone else and there you have the ripple effect. You definitely have touched lives with your book. It was as if time stopped and I couldn't stop reading it. For me, it is very hard for me to find a book like yours somewhere. Chris K., Youngstown, OH

*****

I just wanted to write you a note and tell you what a pleasure it was to meet with you on Sunday. I have very much enjoyed your book and completely agree with the five ways you list as ways to grow stronger in our relationship with God. This week I am visiting friends in North Carolina and I believe your book will be a testimony and a source of inspiration to one of my friends who is doubting the existence of heaven. So once again we experience how God brings God's children together to reach out to someone who is in need of hearing your story in order that they might hear God's story. Thank you for this wonderful ministry! I am already looking forward to your next book. Many blessings, Reverend S.P. +, Brecksville, OH

*****

Confusion and Dilemma

What's the meaning of all the things that I witnessed?

So, I bounced back to my life. Mysteriously, I became terribly ill from where there was no return. Miraculously, I was healed only due to His Grace.

Soon, my doctor released me to my full-time work and, gradually, I returned to all of my other regular activities. This is where my Miraculous True Story supposed to end. But, it did not.

I wrote the first book and it got published on time. But, inside; I was restless. What's the meaning of all the things that I witnessed? Who was this mighty Giant of Pure Light, who mercifully saved me and gave me a second chance? I called Him "Lord", because I automatically knew that He was the Supreme Lord. He needed no introduction. As soon as I saw Him, my knees instantaneously bowed down to Him, and I started to tremble vigorously with fear. I was standing at the far edge of the platform with no railings, where the trembling alone could easily have plunged me into the lake of fire down below. And I knew that would be my permanent death.

The Giant of Pure Light was frightening, but soon, I discovered how loving, how compassionate, how merciful He was to me. How can I ever forget that He has sent me back with very specific instructions? If He didn't do so, I'd have been a forgotten history long ago. But, with the specific instructions came also some responsibilities and obligations that I must finish before He sees me again next time. Next time for me can be any time without any warning.

I found that my background was creating some confusion as well as dilemma for me. Let me share some information about my background with you. I was born and raised in a strong orthodox Hindu family, where both of my parents were devout Hindus. I learned so many things from them. And I am very thankful that God placed me in a family where it was a blessing indeed for me to be raised with the genuine love of both parents. These days it is not so common with new generations. However, as a Hindu, I grew up with the concept of the Heaven and the Hell. Also, I had the concept of the angels. But who is this Divine Giant Lord of Pure Light, whom I encountered? He is unlike any of the Hindu gods or goddesses that I have been familiar with. His face was brighter than the sun I know. His body was radiating with pure Light. His eyes were like blazing fire. I looked at His face once; then I had no courage to look at His face again. I was continuously looking at His feet and pleading for His mercy. His feet were of shiny brass or bronze color. Who is this Lord? I did not know Him; yet He knew me so well; He knew everything about me.

Let me also mention here that all my life I was always proud of my Hindu heritage. The Hindu heritage has a beautiful culture and tradition that goes back to the roots of the Indus Valley civilization tracing back to 4,000 BC. Growing up in that ancient but rich culture, I remember learning many values, not only from my parents, but also from neighbors, teachers and communities. These values have definitely impacted me from my childhood: Values such as honor your father and your mother; respect the elderly; respect your teachers; do not steal; do not tell lies against anyone; do not commit murders; do not commit adultery; do not be greedy to own other people's belongings. Those days I didn't have the slightest clue that these values, which I learned, were almost very identical to the Laws in the Ten Commandments, which God established through Moses for His people in Israel. Now that I'm familiar with the Ten Commandments, it amazes me to think that we were strictly obeying them as Family Rules without knowing the Law of the Ten Commandments. Even today, it is common to see so many sacrifices the Hindu parents make for the sake of their children. It has been a culture where family always comes first. As a result, we see many successful individuals flourishing from this community despite their financial hardship and woes.

For the benefits of some readers, who are not familiar with what the Hindus believe, let me summarize in a few words. Unlike other religions, Hinduism does not comprise of a unified system of beliefs. All we can do is identify the main concepts and expand from there.

Hinduism has a Trinity of three primary Gods. God the Creator is known as *Brahma*. *Brahma* is the impersonal, ultimate Creator of the entire universe. The second person of the Trinity is God the Preserver, known as *Vishnu*. The primary function of the Lord *Vishnu* is to protect creation and life. The third person of the Trinity is God the Destroyer, known as *Shiva*. The primary function of this Lord *Shiva* is to destroy.

However, underneath the three Primary Gods, Hindus believe there are 330 million gods and goddesses whom they worship, as well. Hindus also believe that God is all powerful and omnipresent, but He is beyond us to know Him personally. He is separate from His creation. Only He exists forever. Everything else is *Maya* or illusion. Everything means everything - all except Him in the entire universe is nothing but an illusion. There is no beginning or end in His creation. There are only endless cycles of creation and destruction. The soul in each person is a manifestation of *Brahma*. It appears that the soul is trapped for some reason in the person's body. Only through the repeated reincarnations, is it possible to achieve the ultimate liberations of the trapped souls to be united with the Great soul. This process is called *Moksha* or Salvation. In order to attain the Salvation, Yoga and Meditation are essential steps to follow under the discipleship of a religious teacher or Guru.

After my return from my encounter with the Lord, I had a dilemma that started with my background. Even though I was not a devout Hindu like my parents, I kept wondering why I didn't encounter some sort of Hindu gods or goddesses. The Giant of Pure Light whom I encountered appeared to me as the God Himself. According to my Hindu belief it is impossible to have an encounter with the Creator of the universe. This thought was haunting me all the time. After I returned to my regular activities, I tried to forget the encounter off my mind, but I was not able to erase my experience from my memory.

Another thing that was bothering me was the fact that, when I was zooming in on the faces of the people whom I encountered there inside the Kingdom of Heaven, I was desperately looking for my father and mother. But I didn't see them. It has bothered me ever since, even to this day this makes me very sad whenever I recollect this event. As long as I knew my parents, both of them were very devout, religious, pious Hindus and very good people. If any persons from the Hindu religion deserved to be in the Kingdom of Heaven, I always believed they would. But not finding them there inside, I was not only sad, but also, quite disturbed.

Does that mean that my parents have to go through their repeated cycles of reincarnations according to their faith? Perhaps, some day they would achieve the *Moksha* or Salvation, as the Hindus believe. I kept wondering how and when they'd ever achieve that salvation. I had no way of knowing. Besides, for the Hindu, nobody knows for sure how and when it may or may not happen.

The Hindu faith teaches that the Creator of the universe or *Brahma* is impersonal. Nobody gets to know Him personally. But, the Divine Giant of Pure Light, whom I encountered, I knew instantaneously that He was the Supreme Lord, the Creator of the universe. He was very personal to me. He knew everything about me. He knew all the things that I had done, both good and bad, even though I myself had forgotten some of them, but He didn't.

Another thing that created a dilemma for me was that He didn't send me to another cycle of reincarnation. When I was standing there before Him, I had only two options, either plunge on my left to the deep dungeon dark world with burning flames or be qualified to go through the very narrow door on His left that I witnessed.

There were no other choices for me, such as returning to the life I left behind or getting into another reincarnation.

The only reason I am back to this life is simply because of His Mercy and His Grace. Often, I wonder, why did He have such mercy upon me? Why did He give me a second chance? I was not a sinless person. I committed many sins in my life. Since the wages of sin is death, I definitely deserved to be dead.

I must admit that I was confused for quite some time after my return from the Encounter with the Lord. Even though I wrote the two books per His Instructions, I was still continuously searching for the Truth. What are the meanings of all the things I witnessed? How can I find their true answers? Where can I get them? I was desperately searching for their meanings, as I was seeking the Truth. I needed to know what they meant.

To compound the problem, I had another dilemma that I faced for a considerable period of time. I could not have a dialogue with anyone about the subject matter, except for one or two individuals that expressed genuine interest to know more. At work I was not allowed to discuss any such topic with another person within the facility. Failing to comply with this rule would have caused an immediate dismissal to all parties engaged in such discussions. I could not start a conversation with any of my family members because they lacked the expertise to shed some light on the subject matters. I could not openly discuss with some friends whom I knew because they would have thought that I permanently lost my head resulting from my illness.

However, I desperately needed to know the Truth. Not knowing where to find the answers I turned to the Lord, and I started meditating and praying daily begging for Him to reveal the Truth to me.

Resolution

Relentlessly, I prayed all along for His Guidance and begged Him to show me the Truth and the Way. And, eventually, He did!

He answered all my prayers. Thankfully, I found the Light that I was looking for and, gradually, I found the meaning of everything that I witnessed and much more. Through His Grace, I found my true identity in Him, for which I'll remain ever grateful to Him.

Let me explain how it happened. I believe it was around Easter of 2010 or 2011 when my daughter was asked by one of her friends to participate in a choir group at a local church. When the time came for the actual performance, she asked her Mom and me whether we'd be interested in attending the choir performance by them during the Easter Sunday services. We complied. The name of the church is Grace Church. It is located on Pearl Road in Middleburg Heights, Ohio. I drove by that church numerous times, but I never had the desire to go inside. But here we find again how the Lord works so mysteriously. If it was not for my daughter's singing in the choir group, I'd have never gone inside this church, where the Lord was leading me. I remember the very first time, when I entered this church, I immediately felt His Presence, the presence of the very same Mighty Giant of Pure Light whom I encountered a few years earlier. Also, for me it was the very first time I ever attended an Easter service anywhere.

I looked around the worship area. The auditorium was quite large. It could possibly accommodate more than 1200-1400 people, and the place was completely full. But the atmosphere in the place was exceptionally calm. Senior Pastor Jonathan Schaeffer introduced himself and welcomed everyone. We went through some worship songs. Then Pastor Jonathan started delivering his Easter Sunday sermon. I found it to be truly amazing.

Every bit of the sermon that Pastor Jonathan delivered that morning I felt it was exclusively prepared for me.

How would Pastor Jonathan know what I had been going through for a long time? Again, it felt like he was talking to me directly. I recognized the divine connection. During his sermon, Pastor Jonathan quoted several verses from the Bible. I took note of them. I came home and started looking for the Bible that someone had gifted me about 45 years ago. Unfortunately, it became a totally neglected, as well as a completely forgotten, book. It was collecting dust for all those years. I never had an appetite to read through the contents. Once I tried to read a few pages many years back. But I had to stop because the contents looked so foreign to me. It didn't look anything like my Hindu scriptures that I was familiar with. Since then, it became an abandoned book and remained that way until I started attending Grace Church on a regular basis. It was definitely a sinful situation on my part for many years, and I sincerely regret it now.

So, I managed to find the Bible. I took the dust off and cleaned up the cover pages. For the first time I noticed it was a King James Version. I looked at the verses that Pastor Jonathan was preaching that morning, and I was amazed to discover that the contents in the quoted verses are written exactly the way I witnessed them in my encounter. It was an awesome awakening for me, and from that day onwards I did not miss very many services at the Grace Church. I was hungry to learn more. Also, I kept reading the Bible verses regularly and more frequently. Finally, I started finding all the answers that I was seeking. Everything I wanted to know was all in the Bible. Just like Jesus said, *"Seek and you will find" Matthew 7:7 NIV.* And I did. I must state that my attitude towards reading the Bible has totally changed. Every time I get an opportunity to read the Bible now I delight in it. I have a natural appetite to read more and dig deeper into His Word whenever I have an opportunity. As a matter of fact, now I depend on it every day.

But there was another question that was still bothering me. I needed it to be answered from the scriptures. Who really was Jesus? Some people say that He is a prophet. Others say that He is a good teacher. Some people say that He is Michael, the archangel. Many people from all over the world are adamant in saying that Jesus is no different than any other religious figureheads. According to them, all religions are identical, and they all lead us to the same destination.

The question that was nagging me in my head was: Do they? Do all religions lead us to the same God?

I decided to study the Bible to learn more about Jesus. I started reading the New Testament learning about His birth, His life, His baptism, His mission, His healing of so many people in need, His interaction with His disciples, His teachings, His crucifixion and His resurrection. It was an impressive story; yet He knew everything that was going to happen ahead of time. How was it possible? Why would someone like Him come to this world just to die knowingly in crucifixion, which is the cruelest form of death in my view? And, all along, He knew exactly what He was doing. Over the last few years, I studied the biographies of several religious figureheads, but I never read about any other person like Jesus. I read somewhere that a famous person commented earlier that, once we read the story of Jesus, He must fit into one of these categories. He was either a mad man, or a liar, or a divine person. What category do we think He fits into?

By reading the scriptures, there is no way we can even come close to the notion that Jesus was a mad man. He knew exactly what He was doing. His birth, His crucifixion, His resurrection are all true. Historically, these events have been proven. Why could someone even think that He was a liar, and all the events are not true? The fact that we are writing today's date goes back to the birth of Jesus. Why would the whole world use this date over a period of 2000 years in their calendars if the event was not true?

That leaves us with only one option for us to accept - that Jesus must have been an unusually divine person.

By then, I had other questions that needed to be answered. Is Jesus at the same level as other prophets who came on earth long before his birth, such as Krishna, Buddha, or others? Even several centuries after His birth, one prophet came and claimed to be the last and final prophet. Is this prophet at the same level as Jesus? I needed to know the answer clearly through the scriptures, because many people said to me that Jesus was the same as any other religious figurehead. If that was true, then why didn't I encounter any other religious figureheads when I encountered the Mighty Giant of Pure Light? The answer to this question was very critical for me to know. I continued praying to the Lord for Him to reveal His answer to me, and He did.

In one of his regular Sunday services during November 2011, Pastor Jonathan made an introduction to the author John and his Gospel. That was an eye-opening sermon for me to know exactly who Jesus was through the scriptures. After the sermon, I came home and started reading the Gospel of John, and it was beautiful. I must admit that the Gospel of John is one of my most favorite books in the Bible now. John is so straightforward in his writing. No wonder John was the favorite disciple of Jesus. For anyone who has not read the Bible yet, but has an intention to start, I'd definitely recommend reading the Gospel of John prior to exploring the other chapters.

Here is a summary of Pastor Jonathan's sermon on the Gospel of John and Jesus. Who is Jesus? Jesus is the Word. *"In the beginning was the Word, and the Word was with God, and the Word was God. He was with God in the beginning." John 1:1-2 NIV*

If we replace the Word with Jesus, it will read like this: "In the beginning was Jesus, and Jesus was with God, and Jesus was God. He was with God in the beginning." I exclaimed to myself, it is in writing; it is in the Scripture what I was looking for; Jesus was God Himself. All along I was under the impression that Jesus was just another prophet. Jesus is not like any other religious figureheads. Jesus is God Himself in human form.

The God becomes Human. *"The Word became flesh and made his dwelling among us. We have seen his glory, the glory of the one and only Son, who came from the Father, full of Grace and truth." John 1:14 NIV*

Jesus created everything. *"Through him all things were made; without him nothing was made that has been made." John 1:3 NIV*

Jesus gives us the life. *"In him was life, and that life was the light of all mankind." John 1:4 NIV*

The One and Only is full of grace and truth. *"...Grace and truth came through Jesus Christ." John 1:17 NIV*

There should be no doubt in anyone's mind that Jesus is God Himself in human form. All other religious figureheads that I know of are humans, not God Himself like Jesus. I also believe the Bible is God's Word, and God's Word is always true. God's Word always tells us what is right. Also, God's Word always leads us in the way that is good.

From that day on, I continued attending Grace Church on a regular basis and started reading the Bible as often as possible. After a few years of continued attendance, I decided to be baptized at Grace Church. I made this decision **to follow Jesus.** To follow Jesus is completely different than to be a religious person of any faith. They are two different things diagonally opposed to each other. I intend to discuss this point a little later in this book.

I made the decision to follow Jesus because I knew who Jesus was. He was God Himself.

I find the teachings of Jesus are unlike anything else in the whole world. They are fully divine. I'd also state, if there is such a thing as Absolute Truth, they are to be found in the teachings of Jesus.

Therefore, I decided to remain obedient To Him. This would be my way of expressing my loyalty to Jesus who is God Himself. I was honored to do so at Grace Church on Sunday, April 12, 2015, where I openly announced to the public that I decided to follow Jesus from that day, and I declared Him as the Lord of my life.

This decision to follow Jesus became easy for me only after reading the Gospel of John several times. I became totally convinced that the Mighty Giant of Pure Light, whom I encountered, was none other than the Lord Jesus Himself. He is the One who had the power to save me from my death. He is the One who has given me the second chance. He is the One who healed me and cured me from my ailments miraculously without any medications and procedures. Why did He do that for me? The only answer I can find is that He loves me, although I do not deserve His Love. By the same token, I can say this to all of you that He loves each and every one of us regardless of our religion, culture, or background; the only thing we need to do is seek Him earnestly, and I assure you that we will find Him. Once we find Him, we must accept Him in our hearts. Once we learn how to surrender to Him, we will find that our life will turn to a completely new direction.

I encourage all my readers, who are hesitant, please read the Bible on a regular basis. I've found all of the answers I have been looking for and so shall you. Especially at a time when there are many false teachings, many confusions all around us, it is very difficult to know who is telling the truth or who is misleading the people. The best way is to find the answers by ourselves by reading His word or the Bible on a regular basis. The more we delve into it, the more we get to know the true answers.

What is the Truth?

The truth is: It does not matter who we are. Regardless of our faith and personal beliefs, we must not forget that an eternal bond exists between us as human beings and God, the loving Creator of the entire universe.

Whether we accept the truth or we deny the truth, it does not change the truth. The truth is: God exists today as He existed from the beginning, and He will always exist since He is eternal.

But the harsh reality about us is that we will not exist here for long. God lives forever, but our days on earth are very limited. We are here today. There is no guarantee that we will be here tomorrow or the next day. There is no guarantee that we will live here for another week, another month, or another year.

Yet we hesitate to admit that we are living here on borrowed time. We always like to believe that we are here forever, and much of our behavior throughout our life is a reflection of that belief. We tend to forget that, when our time is up, no one can stop us from departing this world.

Our friends and our loved ones may try their best to keep us here. They may try to obtain the best and the most skilled help to extend our stay on earth for a short while longer, but the truth is: No one can stop us from leaving this world when our time is up. That is why we are called "mortals." We come here to live for a number of years and, when our time is up, we must physically die. We all know it. This is nothing new, and we have no control over this.

Let's pause and think for a moment.

What then would be the purpose of our coming into this world? We come to this earth as an infant; we mature; we work; we live for a few years; and then we die. That's it!

In that case, we would be no different than any other living creature. We can look at all the animals and all the other living species. We can say this is a natural phenomenon. All living creatures must die sooner or later once their cycle of life is complete.

The problem is: We are not like any other living creature. We are definitely not like any other living animal. If we look around, we will find we are unlike any other living species on this earth. We are very unique and quite different. No other living species in the entire world can be compared with us. We are very special.

The characteristics that differentiate us from other creatures are: The power of knowledge and the power of intelligence that we have to apply the knowledge.

If we are determined, we can do almost anything. We have the supremacy over all creatures, not by force, but by the power of our knowledge and our intelligence.

Does it make any sense that unique species like us would come into this world only to live for a few years and then die? Is that the purpose of our life? That being the case, we would be no different than the other species on earth, i.e., animals, plants, etc.

The question would still remain, "For what reason do we have the unique power of knowledge, and why do we have it and not the others?"

What does our power of knowledge say about what actually happens when we die? Does anything happen beyond our death? Does anyone know for sure what goes on after our life ends here? Does everything finish with our death here on earth?

Undoubtedly, these questions have been asked by mankind from the beginning. As a result, there are many theories, beliefs, religions, and cults that have evolved throughout history.

After all these years, they are still present throughout the world today with no major changes. They all have a common theme. "Is there a Supreme Creator?" Most of the beliefs originated from a few eternal questions, such as, "Is there a life beyond our death? If there is something after our death, how can we find the truth?"

Today, if we look into any of these beliefs, we will find that every one of these individual beliefs claims to know the truth whether or not they know the truth. As we look deeper into any one of these beliefs, we will also find that every group truly believes that they are the only ones who know the truth, and all the other groups are totally wrong. Throughout the history of mankind, many wars have been fought to prove one group's supremacy over the others. It is no different today - everyone claims to know the truth.

The question is: If the truth is known to all of these groups, then why do we have so much disagreement, so much friction about the truth? Did we fail to grasp the truth? Could it be that there is more than one truth? Who is right and who is wrong?

It is very puzzling, and, the more we want to delve into it, the more confused we will be. Chances are many of us will never find the truth during our short lifespan in this world.

Is anyone certain of the truth? Has anyone experienced the truth by crossing the border from this world to the other? Has anyone experienced the truth firsthand and returned to tell us what he or she witnessed on the other side?

It is our human nature to have a need to know. We come to conclusions of accepting the truth either through personal experience or scientific proof by experimentation, observation, or documented inference.

By the same token, we also know that this is an absolutely impossible task for us, because we are human beings, and we are mortals. Once we die, that's it. We cannot come back to this world in the same form as we were living prior to our departure.

After all, it is not as if we are crossing the borders from one country to another when we have our passports and visas in order. Upon our return from another country, we can tell others what we experienced there. Today, with our technological advancements, it is not even necessary to physically cross the borders - we can see from our own country what is actually going on in another country.

Why is it that, with so much technological advances, we still do not know for certain if there is a Supreme Creator?

Does He really exist? How does He look? Is there such a thing as afterlife? Is there a place called Heaven? Is there a place called Hell?

If there is a Heaven or Hell, where exactly is it located? How does it look? How can we be sure? Is there any evidence? Why is it that we do not know much about the Supreme Creator, Heaven, or Hell other than what we read in a few religious books here and there?

As human beings, we need to have proof - documents or supporting evidence for everything, similar to when we cross the borders from one country to another country's borders in order to prove that we are legal citizens of a particular country, and we are ok to travel.

But the fact is that we did not need any documents (passports, visas, travel tickets, etc.) when we came into this world; nor will we need any documents when we depart from this world.

Additionally, most of us don't even know if there is a next destination for us. If there is, what would it be like? Will it be a friendly or hostile destination?

After all these decades and centuries, modern science still cannot provide any proof of our next destination. Since there is no proof, it is easy for us to think that our life ends with our death here on earth. And it is not unreasonable for us to think in this way, because it is our human nature. It is unknown territory to most of us. No one knows the answer for certain. Very few people can provide supporting evidence. It is impossible for most of us to go beyond this life, come back, and tell others what is on the other side.

What we think as impossible is not difficult for the Creator, because He is the Almighty One. That is the miraculous true story that has happened to me, as I explained the circumstances in my first book, "Code Blue 99 – A Miraculous Story!"

Much to my surprise, I experienced firsthand that my life did not end with my physical death. I found that my real life started after my physical departure from here. That is the continuation of the "miraculous true story," the main theme of this book.

I consider myself very fortunate to have had the opportunity to meet the Lord face to face and come to know Him very closely. It is only through His Mercy and Grace that He sent me back to the earth to complete my unfinished tasks.

He sent me back with a few specific instructions for me to follow until He sees me again. He also told me to share these instructions with all mankind.

Why has He done so? The only reason is: Divine Love. His love is Pure and Unconditional. I know for sure that He loves me. If He did not love me, I'd not be back on earth to complete my unfinished tasks. I'd have fallen down below into the dingy dungeon that I saw on my left.

I do not know why He loves me. I do not deserve to be loved by Him. I have ignored Him practically all my life. Many times I hesitated to believe whether He truly existed.

But, from my personal encounter with Him, I can assure every reader that He loves you as much as He loves me. He loves and genuinely cares for each and every one of us. The Supreme Creator, whom we call God, does exist. We must never doubt His existence. He is our Heavenly Father, and we can be all His children.

Our relationship with Him is, to some extent, very similar to our relationship with our own physical father. Our physical father may have many children, all of whom are very different. But to our physical father, we are all his children. We are all part of his family. As his children, we are expected to live together and to share our good times and bad times. How different we may be from one another does not make any difference in our father's eyes -we are all equal.

From the very moment of our birth, even though we are very different, we have many things in common.

For example, the first thing we do as a newborn baby is cry. It is very rare to have a newborn baby who does not cry. Crying is a healthy sign. If the newborn baby does not cry, there may be something drastically wrong. It does not matter what religion or background (rich/poor; born at home or in hospital) - the baby must cry.

Why is that so? I am certain there are many scientific and medical explanations for this event. But I think the real reason the baby cries is because he or she has been separated from the secure relationship and ideal place of the mother's womb.

From the period of conception to the baby's birth, the baby experienced the warm security and the genuine love of the mother in the womb. There was a real bond between the mother and the baby that was filled with love and affection.

No one can deny the intensity of love and bondage of a mother for her baby. A mother loves her child so much that she can sacrifice her life for the welfare of her child. With the genuine love of the mother also comes the tender care. The baby felt secure all along, until it is separated from the mother.

From a secured environment, the baby is born into an unknown, very different environment. From the baby's point of view, the new environment is not only different but also a very strange and harsh one.

The only way the baby can express his/her feeling is by crying. The baby continues to cry for that genuine love and tender care he/she felt from the mother. Their relationship continues to be bonded even after the baby is born. Whenever the baby feels the touch and love of the mother, he/she will always become calm. The relationship will continue to grow unless there are other unnatural factors present.

"Can a mother forget the baby at her breast and have no compassion on the child she has borne? Though she may forget, I will not forget you!" Isaiah 49:15 NIV

Ever since we were born into this world, we are continually looking for genuine love, care, and security. Newborn babies find that genuine love and care from their mothers, as well as their fathers.

As we mature, our search continues for genuine love, tender care, and a secure relationship. Sometimes we think we have found them in a relationship, career, or wealth. We spend our entire lives trying to achieve the fulfillment of these attributes of love, care, and secured relationship. If we are fortunate in achieving them, we are relatively happy. Failure to achieve them will definitely make us unhappy and miserable. However, during the process, we tend to forget that our lives here on earth were not given to us to find the secured earthly relationship we worked so hard to achieve. Our lives on earth are very temporary, and we must realize the truth.

All the things we have devoted our lives to acquire are really meaningless. What good is it if we cannot sustain the achievements and acquisition permanently?

The truth is:-When we came into this world we had nothing, and when we leave this world we will take nothing.

So, I'm asking the same question again. What is the truth? - A single God. Does He exist or does He not exist?

Some of you might say, "It may be true for you, but it is not true for me."

Let me reemphasize. Whether we accept the truth or we deny the truth, it does not change the truth. The truth is: God exists today as He existed from the beginning, and He will always exist as He is eternal.

I find this question is also eternal in our heart until we find the truth for ourselves. It is in everyone's heart. Sooner or later, we all will be asking the same question. "What is the truth?" When I read in John 18:38, I find that even the mighty Roman governor Pontius Pilate was asking the same question, certainly under very different circumstances. Here we find that Jesus was betrayed, arrested, humiliated, and brought before the Roman governor Pontius Pilate in connection with the trials and crucifixion. Pilate knew that the charges against Jesus were baseless and not punishable. Pilate did not want to have anything to do with condemning Jesus, and he was having a conversation with Jesus. During their conversation, Jesus admitted that He was a King, and Pilate asked Jesus, "What is truth?" Pilate had no idea what Jesus was referring to. He eventually had the charge against Jesus posted on the cross above his head: **"THIS IS JESUS, THE KING OF THE JEWS." Matthew 27:37, NIV**

The mighty governor looked in the eyes of the Almighty One of the entire universe and asked Him, "What is truth?" Obviously, he didn't recognize Him who Jesus was. Neither did the world. Most people have no idea who Jesus is. I am not an exception either. I didn't recognize Him for a long time. But, now I do. How about you? Do you recognize Him? Who is He really?

Until and unless we come to know who Jesus really is, we will continue with our quest; "What is the truth?"

I invite all my Readers to open John 14:6 and see yourselves what Jesus has to say.

Jesus answered, "I am the way and the truth and the life. No one comes to the Father except through me." John 14:6, NIV

WHAT DOES GOD LOOK LIKE?

This was the most commonly asked question to me after I returned to my second life. I was asked by many people since the first book was published, "Can you describe God? How does He look? Does He look like a human being? Does He have a human face? How old does He look? Is He a Male or Female? What was He wearing?"

I do understand that all of these are natural questions, since we humans cannot see God with our physical eyes.

We always try to rationalize everything with a form, shape, or size to which we can relate.

The question is: How can we relate to someone whom we can never see? He is invisible to our human eyes. Yet He is Omnipresent, present everywhere; He is ever existent; He always was there; He is here now, as you are reading this book; and He will always be everywhere. He is the Number One, the Almighty, and the Spirit of all spirits. There is no one higher than Him.

He is the Creator of the entire universe. Everything in the universe has been created by Him. Therefore, He is the Creator of each and every one of us. The relationship between Him and all of us is: He is our Supreme Father, and we can be all His little children.

Here on earth we may have several fatherly and motherly relationships. But, truly speaking, for each one of us, biologically, there is only one real father and one real mother.

None of us would be here on earth if we were not created by our biological father and mother. Isn't it true? The answer is: Yes. Therefore, our parents are known as our creators.

No one comes into this world without some creators behind them. However, here on earth, for any creation, a male creator and a female creator are needed. Males and Females are limited to the physical bodies and living beings only on this earth.

As the Supreme Creator, the Almighty God represents both males and females. The Almighty God is Spirit. In Genesis 1:27 it is clearly stated, ***"God created man in his own image, in the image of God he created him; male and female he created them."*** He understands and loves both. To God, we are all equal. It does not matter whether we are males or females. We are all His children - His sons and His daughters.

The Truth is: There is One and Only One God. He is a universal God.

The closest thing that I can describe His relationship to us is the relationship of a mother and a new born baby. Just as the relationship between the mother and the child is genuine, so is the love of God for us.

However, God loves and cares for us far more than a mother does for her new born child, because a mother has limitations being a human being. God has no limitations.

He is eternal. He lives forever. He knows each and every one of us far better than we know ourselves. He is present everywhere, yet we cannot see Him. He is Almighty. Nothing is impossible for Him. He can grant life to a dead person. He is a huge Giant. He is a Loving God, and He is Just. He is Pure.

As I mentioned earlier, there is One and only One God Who is the Supreme Father of all living beings. How should we call Him?

Some of us call Him God; some call Him by other names. To God, it does not matter by which name we want to call Him. Some call Him Jehovah; some call Him Lord; others call Him by His different names. I personally prefer calling Him as our Heavenly Father because that is our true relationship with Him. He is our Father in Heaven and we can be all like His small children. To me, His name must represent genuine love and honor for Him and expressing genuine love and honor to Him.

Let's take a look at how we call our physical fathers throughout the world. Some of us call him Dad or Daddy. Others call him Papa, Baba, Abba, Pa, Bapu, etc. There must be hundreds of other names that we call our physical fathers.

Does that make any difference? A father is still a father to his child. The relationship between a father and a child has no bearing upon the names by which we call him, as long as the name bears respect and affection. It is not necessary to call one's father by the name Dad in the region where he is called, for example, Papa.

By the same token, it does not make any difference to God by which name we, His children, want to call Him. The important thing in the name is, when we call our father Dad, Daddy or Papa, etc., that name usually means very close, near and dear one with respect, honor, and love for him. Similarly, when we call God as Heavenly Father, because that is our heart desires, and that name represents respect, honor and love for Him. He knows our hearts and He is ok with that.

One person asked me, "If we know God is living and present everywhere, then why can't we see Him?"

When God created Adam and Eve, they used to see God all the time. God came to see them and they used to discuss things face to Face. That was the way we were created by God in His image that we would be His companions, His children, His friends forever. We were designed and created by God to live in peace, joy and happiness with no death, no suffering, no pain, no sickness or no sorrows. We also know that this relationship didn't last long and we were driven out of His Home because of our foolishness.

The perfect eyes of our first ancestors that used to see God's Face all the time are not available with us any longer. They have been replaced with our physical eyes. In the Bible, we find that Moses is the one who came close to seeing God, even then, we find in Exodus 33:20, God is telling Moses, ***"You cannot see my face, for no one may see me and live." Exodus 33:20, NIV***

Therefore, we cannot see God with our physical eyes any longer because we have very limited vision. We can only see what our eyes are designed to see. We can see most anything within the capabilities of our vision. But, our vision has limitations.

For example, our eyes are not designed to see what an X-ray can see through. Also, our eyes cannot see much when it is dark around us. But, when there is moderate light, we can see clearly. Even in the moonlight we can see more than when it is dark. When the sun is bright and shining, we can see more.

But, with our physical eyes can we look at the sun? We cannot stare at the sun, even for a short period of time. We will be instantaneously blinded if we do so. Our vision on earth has severe limitations.

There are many things we cannot see, but they still exist. We have a tendency to believe that things do not exist if we cannot see with our human eyes. Just because we cannot see something with our human eyes that does not mean that someone or something does not exist.

Modern science and technology have made many things possible for us to see that, traditionally, were not visible to us in the past.

Even with the tremendous progress mankind has made throughout the years, can we still see everything in or around us?

Let's take a look at our own physical body. Can we see everything of which our body consists?

What we see of ourselves is the external shape of our physical body. Modern technology has made great progress. The professionals can now take a look at almost every interior part of our body. They can determine what is wrong and not functioning properly. There is no doubt that human knowledge base has advanced very rapidly. Still then can we see everything?

Our human body is not made of flesh only. We have our mind. We can think. We can rationalize. Can we see our mind? Can we see what goes through our mind at any given moment?

We also have feelings. We feel happy; we feel sad; we feel lonely at times. Can we see what causes us to love or hate someone?

We know that each and every one of us has a soul within us. As long as the soul is resident in our body, we are alive. The moment the soul departs from our body, we are dead.

Can we see that soul? Can modern science or new technology make an image of that soul just to see how it looks? Nobody can see it. But most people know that the soul exists within us.

The life that resides within us is the spirit of God. One can say continuously all day long, "I do not believe in a life; I do not believe in the spirit of God; there is no such thing." Let's pause for a moment. Let's think about the reality.

Whether we believe or we do not believe in the existence of the spirit of God within us, does it matter? Does it change the truth?

The truth is: As long as the life stays within us we can do, think, or say whatever we like. But what happens the moment it departs from our body? We are physically dead. We cannot speak; we cannot see; we cannot feel; we cannot do anything. Whether we believed in our souls or not, it did not matter. We are physically dead. Nothing works. Everything ends physically.

The question is: Does everything end?

God is the Living Spirit of all spirits. Our human eyes are not designed to see spirits.

Each and every one of us is alive, as long as His breath is resident within us.

Can we see the spirit that is living within our own body? If we cannot see the spirit that is living within our own bodies, how can we see the Spirit of all spirits?

The Spirit of all spirits is many times brighter than our sun or any other light we can see. Our human eyes will not be able to withstand His glow and radiance. Our physical body will instantly disappear, if the Spirit of all spirits decides to appear before us in His real form.

We cannot see Him because of our physical limitations. But the Spirit of God that keeps us alive is a part of God. When the life departs the human body, it is in the form of a spirit. Only the spirit that departed our body has the potential to see the Spirit of all spirits.

Throughout our life, many of us keep searching for God everywhere. We always tend to forget that once we invite Jesus who is God Himself in human form as Lord and Savior, His Spirit enters into our body and dwells with us. Then again, He lives so close to us all along, but we can at times fail to recognize His existence within us.

A spirit does not have any permanent physical shape or form. Yet, the spirit can take any form, shape, or size. Not only can the spirits take forms, they can also be living. The primary examples are us. Each and every one of us living in this world is an example of a living spirit inside us. We are all alive because there is a living spirit (the Spirit of God inside us. We are in the billions. Yet there are no two people who will have the exact same attributes. Each one of us has a unique shape, size, and features. We are men and women. Yet we are all different.

As long as the living spirit (the Spirit of God) is resident in our body, we stay alive, and we can do all sorts of things. The minute the living spirit leaves our body, we are physically dead, and we become useless.

Our physical body is left behind to decompose and mix with the soil of the earth.

Everything that we treasure as our own is left behind. We come to this world without any material things and, when we leave this world, we take nothing. Yet we spend our entire life striving for material things.

We live here like "there is no tomorrow." We think that the physical death here on earth is the end of our life. But the spirit that was part of God and left our body at the time of our physical death does not die - it continues its journey. The departed spirit is the real me. It did not die - only the physical body died.

There are countless numbers of spirits, not only here on earth but also in Heaven and other places where we do not want to venture because there are also unclean and nasty spirits.

God is the Ultimate Spirit of all spirits.

I mentioned earlier that the Spirit of God does not have any permanent shape, size, or form that we can define. But that does not mean that the revealed appearance is His only form. When I first saw Him, He appeared to me as a frightening giant, someone who looked tough and meant business. But soon I discovered that He was very loving and very fair.

The truth is: God's spirit in us must leave our physical body when our time is up. After the spirit leaves the body, then only we may be allowed to see Him. But how and in what form we will see Him depends on the purity of our relationship with Him and if we are ready to stand in front of Him.

God the Father is Spirit and cannot be seen by humans. No one has ever seen God the Father, as He said, ***"You cannot see my face, for no one may see me and live." Exodus 33:20 - NIV***

Therefore, we can see Him only through His spirit that dwells in us. Even then, only if we have a pure heart, we will see Him as Jesus said, ***"Blessed are the pure in heart, for they will see God. Matthew 5:8 - NIV.***

Pure in heart means that we have been justified through faith in Jesus Christ through the blood of Jesus.

The more intimate as well as pure our relationship is with Him, the more true exposure of His Spirit we are going to experience. By the same token, we may never see Him if our relationship with Him is not sincere and pure.

He knows who we are and what kind of relationship we are keeping with Him. He also knows what form of His identity we will be able to handle. He will only reveal that much of His identity to us.

God is omniscient. He knows our past, present, and future. He is also omnipresent. He is present everywhere. There is not a single tiny place in the entire universe where we can hide or escape from Him. He is universally fair and eternally divine. There is nothing impossible for Him.

Is God male or female? I was asked that question by many readers.

The Spirit of all spirits is neither a male nor a female. All males and females originate from Him. In Genesis 1:27 we read, *"So God created mankind in his own image, in the image of God he created them; male and female he created them." Genesis 1:27, NIV*

The gender applies to our physical living only, but the Spirit of God inside us is neither a male nor a female.

Just because we humans cannot see God with our physical eyes, we have a natural tendency to doubt whether or not He exists. This is primarily due to our inability to believe (faith) or ignorance about His existence. He is living within all of us. Yet we are looking for Him everywhere.

As soon as we are born to this world, we are instantly influenced by the environments surrounding the places where we are born. Whether we are born into an affluent family or in a slum, into a loving family or in a destructive environment, our upbringings are automatically influenced by the environments in which we live.

As we begin to mature, we are continuously being conditioned by the surroundings of this world. We are constantly being influenced by our parents, brothers, sisters, relatives, friends, neighborhoods, schools, societies, cultures, environments, religions, governments, etc.

As we continue to mature, our life gets tangled into further complications.

The survival of our physical life becomes the primary motto of our life. And, as we continue to struggle for our existence, most of us tend to forget who we really are, and we are getting further and further away from our loving God who genuinely cares for us.

So, to answer the original question, "What does God look like?" my answer is: His true identity can be found only in Christ Jesus. We may never see God the Father, but, we are definitely going to meet God the Son, face-to-Face whether we are ready to meet Him in person or not.

How do I know it? – Because, I was there.

Love Your Family & Love Your Children

At the time when I suddenly came face to Face with God at the Gateway to the Kingdom of Heaven, I found myself trembling terribly with fear, thinking that He would not spare me that day, as I had committed many wrong doings in my life, and I was waiting for His decision about me.

At the same time, I found myself continuously pleading, "Lord, please forgive me for my wrong doings, as I knew not what I was doing. I'm very sorry. Please have mercy upon me." This was true repentance on my part begging Him to forgive my sins. There was no trace of insincerity, it was deeply genuine and it was from the bottom of my heart. Now, I read in Acts 2:38, *"Repent and be baptized, everyone of you, in the name of Jesus Christ for the forgiveness of your sins. And you will receive the gift of the Holy Spirit." - NIV*

I was expecting the worst, but, to my surprise, He said to me, "I'm sending you back to the earth. Go back." Then, He said to me, "When you are back, I want you to love your family and love your children."

The instructions are very simple but very specific and amazingly powerful. Within these two simple instructions, "Love your family and love your children," contain His Guidance, not only for me, but also for each and every one of us. His Guidance is available and critical for everyone regardless of which religion one belongs to. This is how He expects us to live our life here on earth for believers and non-believers. *Love your family and love your children!*

Please note the keyword in the two sentences is Love. What does the word Love mean?

Love means to care, to share, to feel, to express about someone or something. Love originates from God and, therefore, God is Love. When we love someone, we experience God and, if the love disappears in any situation, the experience of God disappears.

God's love for us is genuine, as well as unconditional. He truly loves and cares for us. He wants us to demonstrate the same thing to our family. He expects us to genuinely care for our own family.

How can we demonstrate that we care for our own family?

The very first thing we must demonstrate in any family is to love, as well as honor our father and our mother. If we cannot love and honor our own parents, who raised us from our birth to our maturity, how can we love God?

Let us see what the Bible says about loving our family and what we need to do.

1 "Children, obey your parents in the Lord, for this is right." 2 "Honor your father and mother" – which is the first commandment with a promise - 3 "So that it may go well with you and that you may enjoy long life on the earth." Ephesians 6:1-3 NIV

Specific instructions for every person in the world, indeed!

Our parents are someone we can relate to, associate with, and see; we can feel the compassion and love. We do not see God, and many of us have no clue if He exists or where He resides. How can we love someone whom we cannot see?

Love has to come freely, on its own, from within. One cannot force someone to love.

A family that is united in love is always harmonious, progressive, and happy. The only reason for that is: It pleases God when He sees the genuine love and affection within the family members.

He expects the husbands to love their wives and not to be harsh with them. He expects the wives to love their husbands and to nourish the family with love. He expects the fathers not to provoke their children but to encourage them. He expects the children to obey their parents and love them. Let us see what the Bible says about the rest of the family members. What do we need to do?

18 "Wives, submit yourselves to your husbands, as is fitting in the Lord. 19 "Husbands, love your wives and do not be harsh with them." 20 "Children, obey your parents in everything, for this pleases the Lord." 21 "Fathers, do not embitter your children, or they will become discouraged." Colossians 3:18-21 NIV

Nothing pleases God more than a strong loving family.

It is sad to see the strong family environment deteriorating over the years. Today, we are very busy with many things. We find time for other things, but none or very little time is available for our own family members.

As a result, there are many problems in our families and in our homes. There are many broken homes, broken trusts, and broken relationships in our families. The loving atmosphere has evaporated from many families. In its place, the opposite of love has entered.

As I mentioned earlier, when we love someone, we experience God and, if the love disappears in a situation, the experience of God disappears.

When the experience of love disappears, the opposite force of God enters. The opposite force of love is hate. When hate enters into a family, God cannot dwell in that family, and the evil force sets in instantly without fail.

When we are under the influence of the evil force, we commit more and more wrong doings. Sometimes, we say things to our own family members that can hurt the most.

But, under the influence of the evil force, we may even enjoy hurting the other members of the family.

We must never underestimate the purpose of the evil force. The only purpose of the evil force is to keep us away from God and lead us to destruction.

When that happens, we are basically at the same point where we were at the very beginning of mankind. The evil force was tempting our ancestors to disobey God and they listened to him. Since then, we have been committing many wrong doings, resulting in that we have been getting further and further away from the influence of God.

The further we get away from God, the closer we get to the opposite force of God, the evil one.

Let's take a look at our own families. What is happening in our families today?

We can see with our own eyes, whatever is happening here, that it is not only limited to one corner of the world but is happening everywhere.

More and more families are now following the path of destruction for one reason or another, because the opposite force of love has already entered into our families.

Who is to be blamed for this? We cannot blame anyone else but ourselves.

We are the ones who are responsible for making our own decisions - whether we want to follow love or we want to follow hate.

When we follow the path of Love, we flourish, and, when we follow the path of hate, we must know the consequences that will follow.

Whenever we follow the path of hate, things always go out of control. It is inevitable. But, whenever that happens, we always have a tendency to blame it on God by saying, "Why did you let it happen to me? How could you let it happen to me?"

We forget that God has given us the amazing power of freedom and a free will to choose. It is up to each one of us to decide our fate on our own.

Do we want to experience God, or do we want to experience the opposite of God?

If we want to experience God, then love your family and love your children genuinely. If we want to experience the evil force, then hate your family and hate your children. This is as simple as that.

Allow me to emphasize on this. We must never forget that the only purpose of the evil force is to destroy us. All of the problems that exist today in our families, anywhere in the world, are due to only one reason.

At least one or more of the family members have fallen into the temptation of the evil one, encouraging hate to set in the family. The power of hate is very destructive. Once one falls into the hands of the evil one, it is not easy to be set free.

Just like the little child, who has been taken away by an evil kidnapper from the child's loving home, can never set himself/herself free unless someone with higher authority intervenes or steps in.

But the comforting factor is: God is Love. Even if we want to follow the path of hate, He still loves us. All He wants from us is to come to our senses that what we have been doing is wrong. He wants us to genuinely repent for our wrong doing and return to Him.

If we could only understand that we are being misled to the path of destruction; if only we could ever realize that God would do anything for us in order to protect us from the hands of the evil. If we could simply say to Him, "God, please forgive us for our wrong doings and please show us the way."

If we genuinely ask for His forgiveness, He will definitely forgive us, since He knows: We do not know what we are doing; we are like His small children.

What would we as parents do to our small children when they misbehave? Would we abandon them completely, or would we forgive them?

Most of us would forgive them by knowing that they are immature, and they do not know what they are doing.

In other words, this is Love. We can surrender to Love because it originated from God.

How can we define God's Love?

In our world, love means an intense affection for another person based upon family or personal ties.

We love other people, or we say we love other people, when we are attracted to them and when they make us feel good. When we say we love someone, the truth is that we love that someone conditionally.

In other words, we love someone because they fulfill a condition that we require before we can love them.

When we feel that we love someone but that someone is not fulfilling the condition that we expect out of that person, then the doubt arises whether we really love that someone.

Our love is not only conditional, it is also temperamental.

We love someone depending on our feelings and emotions that can change from one moment to the next. We can be very best friends today, and tomorrow we can be just the opposite - the worst of enemies.

Why is it so? Why do we have enormous mood swings?

It is because we are not maturely developed in our relationship with God and, therefore, we are not perfect.

We need to go back to the basics. We need to start loving our families and loving our children unconditionally. If we cannot truly love our own family members, it would be extremely difficult to love others outside the family.

Why is it that the divorce rate is so high, not only here in America, but also throughout the whole world?

Isn't it true that most marriages did occur in the first place because of the existence of love between the two individuals? Both parties felt they were made for each other, and they were perfect for each other.

Then, suddenly, why do they no longer feel love for each other? Why is it that it is so easy to quit when it happens? It is not only easy to quit, it is also encouraged in our society.

What happened to the marriage vows that we took, "Until death do us part?" Physical death was supposed to part the love. But, more often, we see that the love already departed long before the physical death.

However, in all cases, the departure occurs due to the death of love, not because of the physical death. If we look at it carefully, death of love is the main cause of the death of most marriages.

This is a perfect example of a conditional love. Love only existed as long as the couples were fulfilling the condition of expectations. Once the expectation failed, love immediately ceased.

As a matter of fact, this applies to any of our family relationships, whether the relationships are between the parents and the children or between any members of the family.

The love we demonstrate to each other is nothing but conditional love. The attitude is, "You scratch my back and I will scratch yours. If you do not scratch my back but I scratched yours, then you better watch out. I'm going to show you how I can get even." Isn't that generally the way we react or behave to each other?

Can we ever stop to think what would happen if God reacted the same way with us?

We are all His children or can become His children. Therefore, it would be natural to assume that our Father in Heaven may have some expectations of us.

Are we meeting His expectations?

Certainly not! We continuously fail to live up to His expectations.

Therefore, He has every reason to stop loving us if God was like us

We do that to our own families. Why shouldn't He do so with us?

We look at our loved ones, and, the moment he or she fails to come up to our expectations, we separate/divorce each other. We do not want to keep the relationship any longer. Often we do not even want to see each other.

How can we be so indifferent? Just a short time earlier, we had been so close friends that we could not even think of living without the opposite other.

Don't we think that God has every right to divorce us because we did not fulfill any of His expectations? If it is ok for us, why shouldn't it be ok for God?

We should be ever grateful to God that He is not like us.

The truth is: He does not stop loving us every time we fail to fulfill the condition of His expectations. He still loves us the same. It does not matter how many shortcomings we have. He still loves us the same. This is called unconditional love.

Will we ever be able to love someone unconditionally? How about our own family? Will we ever be able to forgive the shortcomings of the other persons, whether they are our spouses, sons and daughters, or our parents or siblings, the persons who are very close to us?

If we could, then there would be no separations, no divorces, no arguments, and no hatreds between our loved ones. Why can't we be like that?

God is doing that to us every time, every day. We are all created in the image of God. We should be able to do that. But did we ever try to forgive and accept the other person? Perhaps we can try a little harder through the power of the One who strengthens us to do His will.

Many of the problems we see in today's families are due to only one reason - lack of unconditional Love – the attribute of the presence of God in our lives.

We cannot love our spouses unconditionally. We fail, and we have broken marriages. We cannot love our parents unconditionally. The parents, who gave up their entire life to bring comfort and security to their children, we cannot love them.

Often we cannot stand our own parents near us. When they need our help and support the most, we leave them to live their final days in the world with loneliness, with miseries, with broken hearts and with pain and agonies. Sometimes we think that they deserve to live their life in solitude. Why do we think that way? Because we fail to recognize that our love to our parents has not been genuine, rather it was conditional. We have not been able to love them unconditionally.

By the same token, some of the parents may think that we love our children unconditionally. But do we? How many of us rejoice when our sons and daughters turn 18? Why? Is it because we love them unconditionally?

How can we really comprehend unconditional love? It seems the love that mothers have for their small children is as close to the unconditional love as we can get.

It is true that most mothers continue to love their children through good times and bad times, and they do not stop loving them even if their children don't meet the expectations they may have of them.

We make a choice to love our children, even when we consider them unlovable; our love doesn't stop when we don't feel love for them.

This is similar to God's love for us. But, as we shall see, God's love transcends the human definition of love to a point that is hard for us to comprehend.

God is Love, and His love is very different from human love. God's love is unconditional, and it's not based upon feelings or emotions. He doesn't love us because we're lovable or because we make Him feel good. He loves us because He is Love, and He created us to have a loving relationship with Him, as well as with our own families.

We can see the power of love in our daily life. When a child is born to a family, the child is instantly loved by the parents and other family members.

A mother's love to an infant is unquestionable. A father's love and dedication to provide the best for his child is similar to what God can provide for us as His children.

The difference is our efforts in this world are limited to our means, whereas His efforts are endless and have no limits.

There is no doubt that Love has to be the fundamental basis of our life. God expects us to live lovingly.

We must go back to the basics and start demonstrating love to the members in our own family. All members in a family must love each other.

As long as the mutual love exists, the family remains united, prosperous, happy, and joyful. It does not matter whether it shines or rains in the family, the members will remain together because of love and care.

What is our understanding of a family?

Typically, a family includes today the parents and the children only.

But, in the broader sense, family also includes other family members, such as uncles, aunts, grandfathers, grandmothers, and many other members of the family. Actually, a group of people who are blood-related and having the same identity are usually considered a family.

But, in today's world, most family members are scattered in various places. It does not matter how scattered we are, the word, "home," always brings to most of us the memory of unity, joy, sharing, and caring.

Home and Family are inseparable.

Whenever we say the words, such as "home" or "family," that automatically means it is the place where we are loved; where we are safe; where we are united; where we are trusted; where we belong.

A family brings the pride, identity, and joy to our individual life. A family also means where our ancestors were; where we are today; and where our future generations will be.

The one and only way to keep our home and family alive and secured is through love. God expects us to love our family members. He expects us to care for them. He wants us to share our happiness and our sorrows with one another. He wants us to help each other, comfort each other.

Why does He want us to love our own family first?

Because our family is our very own; our family members are very near and dear to our hearts. Parents need to love each other first before they can love their own children. Children need to love and respect their parents first before they can learn to love others.

As I said earlier, love cannot be a forced attribute. It has to come freely from within, such as a mother's love to her infant.

The word, "Love," is the very fundamental basis of God's expectations of us in this world.

They have been repeated numerous times over the years - "Love One Another;" "Love and Honor Thy Parents;" "Love Thy Neighbor;" "Love Yourself;" "Love Your Family;" "Love your God;" etc., etc.

I know for sure God loves me.

Otherwise, He would not have sent me back to the earth with His instructions.

I also know that He loves each and every one of us and He is like the devastated father of the lost child who has been taken away from the child's home.

He is anxiously waiting for us, His lost children, to come back to Him and live with Him, enjoying the eternal love, peace, happiness, and joy as one happy family.

Where can we find Him?

Where Can We Find God?

I remember, when I was very young, my father once told me a story about a man who was confined in a large building practically all of his life.

He said, "The building can be compared to a prison having four walls and one window." Whenever the man felt lonely, he would stand at the window. Through the window he could see everything of the outside world, and, to him, that was his entire world.

Sometimes, he would spend hours standing at the window, looking at the trees, the birds, and the clouds. Sometimes, he would look at the sunrise in the morning, other times the sunset, once in a while the rain, and thunderous storms. That was his world, and he was content with his knowledge of the world. If someone asked the man to define the world, he would define it based upon whatever he had seen through his prison cell window.

Then, my father asked me if that was the perimeter of the world the man was describing. At that time I was a student in middle school and had studied some history and geography. I quickly said, "No, father! That's not the perimeter of the world. The world is much bigger than what that man was describing. I've studied in my geography books that the world includes Asia, Europe, Africa, America, and Australia."

My father gave a smile to my answer and said that the world is actually much bigger than even that. "Keep on seeking the real answer, and someday you will find the truth."

At that time I was very young, and I did not comprehend how the world could be much greater than what I knew through my history and geography books.

Now, I began to realize that each and every person in this world is like the confined prisoner my father was telling me about. We think we know a great deal. Sometimes we feel that we know everything.

But the truth is: The world is much bigger than what we know, and, the more we know beyond this earth, the larger the world becomes. We know there is a vast universe, and we are just like the confined prisoner in that prison cell. Our knowledge of the vast universe is very limited.

Our vision of the universe is whatever we discovered thus far. However, there is a difference between discovery and invention. Every time someone accidentally discovers something new, we tend to say that so and so invented this newly found item.

The truth is: Everything that we say someone invented was always there, whether it is a new medication, new technology, or anything else. Those things always existed, and we are just discovering them as we expand our horizons.

Our knowledge base is expanding rapidly. There is no doubt about that. Never before, in the history of the mankind, has the knowledge base been so advanced.

We live in an era of Information Technology, and every bit of information is available on our fingertips. Practically anything on any subject we want to know is instantly available.

Yet, we live in a world where most of us are getting more confused, more uncertain of what's going to happen next.

Why is it that many people are getting vastly confused, while our knowledge base is rapidly expanding?

As we expand our knowledge base, we seek to know more. It seems it is a never-ending quest to know more. It seems we are never happy with our knowledge base. The continuous thirst for knowledge increases, yet we feel more and more insecure.

At times, we feel very lonely, as if something is missing in our lives. We become restless. We cannot be at peace with ourselves. We will not calm down, not until we find the truth.

The truth is: We are lost in this world. We must find the way back to our real home, where our eternal Father is anxiously waiting for us.

Where can we find our eternal Father?

We seek Him in all the places where we think we will find Him. We are anxious to find Him, yet we cannot be sure if we really know where He is.

The main reason we cannot find God is because we search for Him everywhere, except where He resides. We look for Him everywhere, but we cannot find Him because we overlook where He resides.

He is residing in each and every one of us. If we seek Him, we shall find Him. I still remember what my father once said to me, "Keep on seeking the real answer, and someday you will find the truth."

But my problem was - I never thought it was necessary for me to seek Him. Like most of us, I was too busy with my day-to-day life.

We live in a world where our daily life is constantly on the move. If we are not capable of maintaining the same speed of the daily life, we fall behind. Everyone else is moving ahead, except the one who is not moving. The one who is not moving along is quickly falling behind.

Today, we cannot just think of one thing at a time. We live in a time where we are constantly being pulled in multiple directions. We are all trying to be experts in multiple areas. Everywhere, singular tasking has already become a thing of the past.

In order to succeed in life, we need to be able to do multiple tasks at the same time. We no longer have time to devote to one single item. We are constantly busy, and our lives are getting busier. The faster our lives get, the more day-to-day activities are needed from us for our survival or physical existence.

Whether we like it or not, we feel that we have no choice but to go with the mainstream flow.

We are afraid that we will find ourselves labeled "unfit" for the mainstream survival. By and large, generally speaking, most of us as average people have lost the meaning for the real purpose of our lives.

If someone asks: "Where are we headed?" the answer surely would be, "We do not know." We are all moving fast, but we do not know what our destination is.

Some of us may even say, "Who cares? We only have one life. When we are dead we go six feet under. That's it. Let's live our life! Why worry?"

I used to think that way too - our life comes to an end when we depart from this world. Therefore, we must live and enjoy to our fullest, as long as we are alive.

It is not unusual for many of us to believe that here on earth every human being is for himself or herself. Our life and the wellbeing of our life is the most important concern to us.

We do not see anything wrong to be selfish. Our logic was that nobody really cared about us. Therefore, why should we care about somebody else?

We struggled, and we earned our living. As long as we have food on our plate, we are happy. If someone else is starving for a piece of bread, that is not our problem.

As long as we have a roof over our head, we feel secure. If someone else is desperate for shelter in bad weather, that is not our problem. Let him earn his living, just like we did ours. Why should we worry about someone else's problem?"

That is generally the way the majority of us think today and reasonably so. We are taught from our childhood that we ourselves are the most important person in our life. Everyone else comes second.

Is there anything wrong with this logic? What do we think?

Let me ask - how would we feel if our parents had that very same attitude towards us? Where would we be today? Would we be the same person we are now?

Where would we all be, if God took the same attitude towards us?

Let me assure you that the above logic is totally against God's principle.

The objective of our life in this world is to live lovingly. First, we need to learn how to love our family and how to love our children. Then, we also must learn how to love others.

God helps those who are compassionate toward others, who are less fortunate than we are. We cannot serve God unless we can serve others.

So, where do we find God? Where should we look for Him?

To which temple should we go to find Him? Which church should we attend? To which religious place should we pay a visit?

Once we go to the temples or churches or any other religious places: How can we be sure that He is there?

How can we be in sync with Him?

Let me emphasize that we will not find God in any of the usual places where we have been searching for Him.

First, we need to seek Him through our heart. God wants us to find Him there in our heart.

Jeremiah 29:12-14 NIV states, 12 "Then you will call on me and come and pray to me, and I will listen to you." 13 "You will seek me

and find me when you seek me with all your heart". 14 "I will be found by you" declares the Lord, "and I will bring you back from captivity."

God created us in His Image for the purpose of having a personal relationship with each and every one of us. But we fell into the traps of the Evil One and became his captives. Ever since, we are continually falling into the temptations and, as a result, we are going further and further away from Him. But He still pursues us. He still loves us. He still longs for us. He wants us to know Him.

Fortunately, He has not forgotten us or abandoned us. Anyone who wants to find Him through his/her heart, He is not that far away from anybody.

27 "God did this so that they would seek Him and perhaps reach out for Him and find Him, though he is not far from any one of us." 28 "For in him we live and move and have our being" Acts 17:27-28, NIV

So, where can we find God? - Not in the temples, not in the churches, not in the synagogues, not in the mosques, nor in any of the religious institutions. He wants to dwell in our hearts. He is longing for a one-on-One personal relationship with every one of us. What kind of a personal relationship is He longing for? – A sincere one, a true one and an honest one, a genuine one, not an artificial one, nor a fake one.

How are we going to do that? We do not even know who God is or what He looks like. He made it very easy for us.

Nobody has seen God the Father. But God Himself came down to the earth as a human. We call Him God the Son. He is Jesus Christ. He is God Himself in human form. He came down and lived a sinless life. Willingly He gave His life in crucifixion so that we can have an eternal life.

Who would do anything like this unless this person is a mad man or God Himself in human form? Do you believe He was a mad man? I do not think so because I met Him in person face-to Face. I found Him full of Mercy, full of Grace, and full of Love. It is beyond my comprehension why He still loves me. I have nothing to brag about me. I definitely do not deserve His Love.

However, if we believe in Jesus, we have to accept the fact that He was not a mad man but God Himself in human form. Then let us listen to what He is saying to each and every one of us.

"I am the way and the truth and the life. No one comes to the Father except through me. If you really know me, you will know my Father as well. From now on, you do know him and have seen him."
John 14:6-7, NIV

Does anyone still have any doubt who Jesus is or where can we find God?

Religions and God

There are many different religions and quite a few different cults in the world today. I'm not a spokesperson for or against any religion. I believe that most religions originated with the idea of finding God and how to reach to Him. I also believe that many of these religions were either created by influential people or a group of like-minded people in order to guide the ordinary people in finding the truth.

From the beginning, mankind was aware of the existence of a supernatural power and, keeping that in mind, various religions had evolved throughout different corners of the world. Each religion had its own unique approach as to how to reach God.

Ironically, each one claims to be the only true religion in the world. In other words, each one claims that all the other religions are wrong, and they are the only one that is right. If we look back throughout history, we will find more wars were fought over religion than any other issue.

The primary motive to fight any of the religious wars was to establish that one religion is superior to the others. Today, it is not much different.

Every religion is working diligently to convince people to be religious. Every religion's primary motto is to increase the number of religious people of the same faith. There are so many factions, so many denominations, and so many beliefs, that one can easily get confused in trying to decide who is right and who is wrong.

I must confess that I'm not a Theologian, and I'm not qualified to talk about any religion. I've not studied any of the religious books diligently. Therefore, I'm not going to say I'm in favor or against any religion. Religions serve their own purpose.

It is not my intention to convert anyone to any particular religion. My purpose in writing this book is only to share His specific instructions that were given to me, and I was asked to share them with all mankind.

When I was face-to-Face with God and He was sending me back to the earth until He'd see me again next time, I was continually pleading to God, "Please, Lord! Please guide me to prepare myself for the next time. When I'm back to the earth, please tell me which church I must join, which temple, or which synagogue. If you want me to join any religious institution or association or any other place, I will join whatever You say, but please guide me."

Initially, God didn't respond. But, after repeated pleadings, the Lord said to me, "No, it is not necessary for you to join any church, any temple, or anything else. Those things are not important to Me."

I must admit that I was initially very much shocked to hear this from Him.

From my childhood, I was under the impression that the more religious a person is the more he/she will be closer to God, and God will really favor that person. Now what I heard from Him was mind-boggling to me.

Why did the Lord say that religions are not important to Him? -

It is because there is no religion in the world that has the authority or power to hand over one lost soul to the Kingdom of Heaven.

Yet, if we look around, we will find that every religion is fierce in claiming that it is the only way to reach God.

Isn't it sad to see so much bloodshed in the past and present over the supremacy of a religion when God, Himself, is saying, "Those things are not important to Me?"

The Lord continued, "What is important to Me is your personal relationship with Me – I want to see how sincere, how honest, how true are you with Me? That's the only thing that counts."

It is very clear, from His Guidance, what should be the most important priority for us. It does not matter to which religion or faith we belong. Your religion, and religion in general does not and will not save you.

As an individual, the most important priority for us should be to have a sincere and honest personal relationship with God. It is completely different than being a "religious" person.

When the appropriate time comes, I am sure each one of us will experience the face-to-Face conversation with Him. To the contrary of our belief, we will then discover that God is neither Hindu, nor Buddhist, nor Christian or Jew, nor does He belong to any particular religion that exists today.

Those of us who will face Him one day will be very much surprised to discover that God does not belong to any specific religion. He is a Universal, Loving God, and He belongs to all mankind, regardless of our belief, what we call ourselves; Hindu, Buddhist, etc.

He is our Heavenly Father, and we are all His children. He created us in His Image. In return, what did we create?

We, His children, are the ones who created many images of Him.

What kind of a relationship does God want with us?

He wants a relationship that is totally sincere, completely honest, and absolutely true.

Does any religion have the authority to hand over that relationship from an individual directly to God on behalf of that individual?

Not really; not at all. It is up to us, each individual, to build that personal relationship with Him.

Let me explain one thing from my own experience. When I was there in front of Him face-to-Face, I was totally alone. There was no one else to help me. I had to speak for myself.

Similarly, when anyone of us is going to be there facing Him, we will have to deal with Him on an individual basis.

We will be responsible for our own actions, inactions, wrong doings, and attitudes, whether good or bad. We will be all alone, one-on-One. There will be no religion there accompanying us or to help us.

We are responsible for our own acts, and we have to answer to Him ourselves. When we come to this world, we come alone, and when we depart this world, we will depart alone. No religion or places of worship will go with us.

Yet many of us will spend our entire lives attempting to be strictly a religious person of a particular faith. We can do anything in the name of religion; we can make sacrifices; we can fight wars; we can kill others, all sorts of things.

Why do we do that? - Because we want to go to heaven, and we want to please God so that we can be with Him.

But God Himself is saying, "Build an honest relationship with Me, one-on-One, true and sincere."

And where is He? He is inside you and me. He dwells in our heart. He is there with us day and night.

All we need to do is open our hearts to Him. We do not need to go to any temples or any other religious institutions to do that.

We can go to any of our religious centers daily, devote all sorts of time and money, and do all kinds of things for ourselves or others, and that won't make any difference to Him, as far as we are concerned. They are meaningless, unless we can build a totally honest, sincere, and true relationship with Him.

How do we build a relationship with someone, and how can we make that a long-lasting relationship?

There are a few ingredients that must be present in order to build any type of serious relationship.

The same ingredients apply to any relationship, whether it is with our own family members or with someone else. They are: love, trust, and commitment.

Love is the primary factor that must be present in any type of long-lasting relationship. Then we must trust each other. And finally, for us to grow the relationship, we must be committed.

Whether it is a relationship between two spouses, between parents and children, or between any other members of society, these three factors must be present to build and to sustain a long-lasting relationship.

If we lack in any one of these attributes during the process, the relationship breaks down. As long as love, trust, and commitments are there, the relationship stays on solid foundation.

It is no different when it comes to building a relationship with God. First, we must love Him; then we must trust Him; and then we must stay committed to Him.

How many of us can truly say, "I love you God, and I love you more than I love myself?" How many of us do sincerely trust Him and, reciprocally, He can trust us to remain faithful? How many of us can say, "God, you can count on me every time. I'm committed, no matter what?"

Similar to any relationship, this may start at a thinner scale and, as the relationship matures, it will solidify. However, the desire for forming a personal relationship with God must come first freely from within us.

Each one of us must initiate that process; each one of us must seek that personal relationship with Him. Once the desire is felt and we are aware of the fact that part of God is resident within us, we must invite God's Spirit to help us grow in the relationship.

But, all the tasks and changes within us must be done by us. No religion can do it for us on our behalf.

As humans, we definitely need a support group to help us through our difficult times, remind us of the need for coming to God, teach us in the ways of the Lord, and assist us in accomplishing His directives.

We can all relate to automobiles. For example, we want to go from point A to point B.

How do we go there? We can go there by the use of a vehicle. But the vehicle alone cannot take us from point A to point B. Each vehicle will need a driver to drive the vehicle and control it until we safely arrive at our destination.

A religion can be compared to the vehicle. That vehicle is a necessary medium to help us get to our destination. But the driver of the vehicle is in control of where we are going.

In our case, we individuals are in control of determining where we will be going. We are like the individual driver of the vehicle. We are responsible for our own destiny, and religions are tools to assist us.

When we are there in front of Him, no one else can help us other than God Himself. I stood there on the platform and met Him face-to-Face from where He sent me back to the earth. From my own personal experiences, I can clearly state that the only two individuals who will be there are He and you.

Therefore, it is for our own sake that we seek God in ourselves and find Him amidst our busy life. Once we find Him, we must start establishing a meaningful relationship with Him. And in order to do that we must demonstrate our honest love, sincere trust, and true dedication to Him.

The question is: "How do we get started? Where do we begin?

We are constantly being distracted by our enemy, the evil one, who is determined to prevent us from reaching our goal. He will do everything in his power to keep us away from God.

It is true that we have been living under the shadow of darkness for a long time. We think we know the Truth, but, truly speaking, we do not know the Truth.

The truth is: We have been lost. We cannot find our way back to our real home. We are living under the captivity of the darkness for a long time. We are being exploited by various groups. We are confused.

We do not know what to do. We are like the little child who was taken away as captive, rendering him unable to find his way back to his real home. Someone with higher authority must intervene to free him. If the child's father knows his location, would he not do anything in his power to get his son back?

Fortunately, God is Omniscient. He knows everything. He knows us more than we know ourselves. He knows our sorrows. He knows our weaknesses. He cares for us so much that He Himself came down to live with us as human in order to rescue us from our path of destruction.

When He lived among us, He lived a perfect life. He showed us how to live our life on earth lovingly. God loves us so much that He gave His own human life for us, so that we can have eternal life with Him. We should never doubt that He was God Himself in the form of a man.

Let me assure you that God didn't do it for any particular group of people or for any specific religious group of people. He did this for all mankind, regardless of our faith or background.

All we need to do is believe in Him wholeheartedly.

"For God so loved the world that he gave his one and only Son, that whoever believes in him shall not perish but have eternal life." John 3:16, NIV

Who is God's one and only Son? He is Jesus Christ, God Himself in human form, our only Savior who can save us from our captivity in darkness. He is the One I met face-to-Face. He is the One who is the Mighty Giant of Pure Light that each one of us will stand face-to-Face after our physical death here on earth. No religion of any kind can save us from the bondage except the God Himself. Let us see what Jesus (God Himself in human form) is saying to His disciples in John 14:1-6

Jesus is comforting His Disciples. *1 "Do not let your hearts be troubled. You believe in God; believe also in me." 2 "My Father's House has many rooms; if that were not so, would I have told you that I am going there to prepare a place for you?" 3 "And if I go and prepare a place for you, I will come back and take you to be with me that you also may be where I am." 4 "You know the way to the place where I am going." John 14:1-4, NIV*

In the following verses Jesus (God Himself in human form) is very specific with His instructions to us in what we need to do.

5 Thomas (one of the Apostles) said to him, "Lord, we don't know where you are going, so how can we know the way?" 6 Jesus answered, "I am the way and the truth and the life. No one comes to the Father except through me". " 7 If you really know me, you will know my Father as well. From now on, you do know him and have seen him." John 14:5-7, NIV

I am asking the same question again to every one of my Readers. Do you think that Jesus was a mad man, or a liar, or God Himself in human form? The decision of "who Jesus is" rests entirely up to each individual.

I know He is the Creator of the universe, and He is telling the truth. I know it for sure because I met Him face-to-Face, and He mercifully saved me, giving me a second chance. I was blessed.

As a Creator of the universe, He does not need to tell us anything. He does not owe us anything. The only reason He is telling this to us is because He loves us so dearly. He does not want any of us to perish. He wants everyone to come to Him, regardless of our religions, culture, or background. He loves us so much that He gave His human life for us. But, if any of my Readers really believes that Jesus was not God Himself in human form, then Jesus must fall in the category of either a mad man or a liar. Please think of it twice before you make that decision for yourself.

Each person is entitled to make his/her own decision. That's why God gave us our own free will. He does not force anyone to love Him. The decision to love Him must come from within.

Out of our own free will, we all need to make that decision whether we want to accept or reject Jesus. He is knocking on our door. Do we want to believe in Jesus or do we want to believe in our own Religion? Do we want to accept eternal life or do we want to accept eternal death? The decision is entirely up to each one of us. There is no other alternative.

Believeth in Me!

God, in His human form, said to us, **"Whosoever _believeth_ in Me shall have everlasting life."**

He also said, not everyone who says, "Lord! Lord!" will enter into the Kingdom of Heaven.

"Not everyone who says to me, Lord, Lord will enter the kingdom of heaven, but only the one who does the will of my Father who is in heaven" Matthew 7:21, NIV

Therefore, "Believeth in Me" must have a special meaning, I do not think that it means a superficial belief, a temporary belief, or a belief as we find convenient.

"Believeth in Me" can be compared to how a little child believes in his/her parents as instructed by Jesus Himself in Matthews Chapter 18 below.

1 At that time the disciples came to Jesus and asked, "Who, then, is the greatest in the kingdom of heaven?" 2 He (Jesus) called a little child to him, and placed the child among them. 3 And he said: "Truly I tell you, unless you change and become like little children, you will never enter the kingdom of heaven." Matthew 18:1-3, NIV

Jesus is saying that we who believe in Him must become like little children. What does it mean?

A little child completely depends on his/her parents. A little child truly believes that with the parents he/she is very safe, loved and nourished. When the child believes in his/her parents, there is no doubt, flaw, or hesitation. It is a pure and complete faith. From the child's point of view, that's all he/she knows; that's all he/she trusts; and that's all he/she is committed to.

Unfortunately, there are many among us who say, "Lord! I believe in You!" But, when we look into their belief a little deeper, we will find their belief is only for a temporary period of time - perhaps once a week for a few hours or maybe two or three times a week, or whenever it is convenient for them. The rest of the time many of us act as if we do not know Him at all. Perhaps it would be more appropriate to say that we believe in Him whenever we feel it is convenient for us.

As a matter of fact, many such believers turn around and do everything that is contrary to His commands. We behave as if He does not exist. Many of us fall into this category, and we can be classified as either superficial or part-time believers, not knowing what "believeth in me" means. That is not the way "believeth in me" is meant to work. Whenever we say we believe in Him, it must be a genuine belief, not a superficial or fake one.

The issue here is similar to what He said to me. He wants to see my personal relationship with Him one-on-One. He wants to see how sincere, how true, and how honest my relationship is with Him all the time. That's what it means by the words, "Believeth in me."

I know it is rather difficult for us to be a full-time believer. In this world, we are constantly being pulled into two opposite directions - good and evil. Both are powerful forces. But we must not forget that good always triumphs over evil in the end.

Although part of His Spirit is living within us, God gave us ultimate freedom to choose on our own which path we want to follow - good or evil.

If we choose to believe in good, He will protect us from the hands of evil and lead us to the way. But, if we choose the path of destruction, He is not going to say, "No," to us, because that's a decision we are making on our own. Therefore, we must accept the consequences for our own deeds.

He does not force us to choose to love Him. That decision must come naturally from within.

Once we come to the self-realization that we could become children of God and we are lost here on earth, we must also realize that we are constantly under the influence of the Evil One. Especially those of us who say we believe in Him, the Enemy will come out forcefully to test the depth of our belief. If the Enemy finds we are in a shallow depth of our faith or belief, he might leave us alone because we are not much of a threat to his power and control. We are still easy targets for him when it comes to his temptations. We must never forget for a moment that we are not exempt from the temptations of the Evil One just because we say, 'I believe in You, Lord!' We will find it is to the contrary.

The Evil One will always tempt us to commit all sorts of wrong doings. Once the wrong doings are committed by us, whether we want to commit them or not, we must be penalized for our acts. There is not a single sin that gets unpunished. The only way to be forgiven is to genuinely repent for our wrong doings and come to the Lord begging for His forgiveness as soon as possible. This is no different here on earth among our family members.

Whenever our children do something wrong and come to their human fathers, genuinely expressing their mistakes and saying I am sorry, any human father will forgive them.

God is much more loving than the human fathers. He will undoubtedly forgive us our wrong doings, if we can truly say, "We are sorry, God. Please forgive us. We will not commit the same mistakes again. Please help us."

However, we should not continue doing the same mistakes over and over again and ask repeatedly for His forgiveness towards the same mistakes. After a few repeated times, it will be apparent that we are not genuine in our relationship with Him. We must not forget that He knows us much better than we know of ourselves.

Like the young child who was lured away and unable to free himself from the evil person on his own, we cannot free ourselves from the influence and the temptations of the Evil One on our own. The Evil One is powerful, and he is always tempting us to commit wrong doings. The young captive child can only be freed if there is some intervention by a higher authority, such as police or the father, himself, along with his friends.

Similarly, we cannot free ourselves from the hands of the Evil One without the help of higher authorities. In our case, we need divine intervention, the Holy Spirit, to free us from the influence of the Evil One. Without the Holy Spirit, most of us are not strong enough to resist the evil on our own.

God knows our situation. He loves us so much that He Himself came down to this world in order to defeat the Evil One and save us. We must accept the fact that He came down on earth and gave His human life for us. The only thing we must do is believe in Him, not superficially but genuinely, not part-time or as we feel convenient, but all the time, 24 hours a day, seven days a week, year-round.

Our rescue from our bondage to the Evil One is only possible if we can genuinely place our trust in Jesus, and we must remain faithful to

Him at all times. We must not forget that the Evil One is going to tempt us and raise our doubts about Him. But we must remain steadily obedient to Him.

We must remember that those who claim salvation but don't obey Him are not truthful to Him. The obedience comes from complete faith in Him. For God did not call us to be impure but to live a holy life. Therefore, he who rejects this instruction to be faithful in Him rejects God.

If we genuinely ask God to help us, He always sends us His Holy Spirit. Without the help from His Holy Spirit, we will not be able to withstand the hands of evil. Once we place our trust in God, His Holy Spirit will guide us as to how to live on earth according to His instructions.

Once we accepted His Holy Spirit to come into our hearts, we can no longer be a part-time believer in God. Our faith in Him must grow to be a constant believer, not just whenever it is convenient for us.

As we mature in our relationship with Him, we will notice a big change in us. We are not the same person any longer. The objective, therefore, for each one of us is to grow our personal relationship with Him. Our personal relationship with Him must be true and honest. We cannot say, for a short while, "Lord! Lord!" And then turn around and do just the opposite. Then we are not true to Him.

We must always remain truthful to Him. We must always tell the truth. We cannot tell lies. Many of us have tendencies to tell lies, and many people think that it is an acceptable practice in our society. It may be acceptable in our society but not to God.

In order to be sincere with God, first we must be sincere and true to ourselves. This is the first instruction He asked me to obey and share with everyone. It does not matter to which faith we belong. We must remain truthful to ourselves so that we can remain truthful to God.

He instructed to me, **"Always Tell the Truth! Do not be afraid to tell the Truth."**

This is a fundamental step in building our personal relationship with Him. It sounds like a very simple instruction. But it is not so simple to keep. How many of us can truly say, not being face-to-Face with Him, just to ourselves, "I always tell the Truth. I'm not afraid to tell the Truth?" – Most probably none.

Let's pause for a moment. Why is it so difficult for us to tell the Truth?

I know for many of us it is so easy and comfortable to tell lies.

Telling lies does not come from the Positive Force. Telling the Truth comes from the Positive Force.

When we are telling lies, are we under the influence of Positive or Negative Force? If we are under the influence of Negative Force, we are acting completely opposite to what God wants. In that case, how can we ever be in sync with God?

Therefore, the very first step in our relationship with Him is: "Tell the Truth, and do not be afraid to tell the Truth."

If it appears to be too difficult for some of us to tell the Truth, my suggestion is to try surrendering to Him and seeking His help. He is always ready to help anyone from any religion who is sincerely asking for His help. To Him, we are all His children. It does not matter to which religion we belong.

The next instruction from Him was: **"From this day on forward, commit no more sins!"**

What did He mean by the word, "sin?"

To me, sin is the same word as wrong-doing. There is no difference. Sin means an action that is prohibited by the Divine Entity. Sin also means an action that is considered wrong. Sin refers not only to physical actions taken but also to thoughts and internal motivations and feelings. Any thought, word, or act considered immoral, shameful, harmful, or alienating may be termed "sinful."

Apostle Paul explains The Law and Sin beautifully in Romans chapter 7, as stated below.

14 "We know that the law is spiritual; but I am unspiritual, sold as a slave to sin. 15 I do not understand what I do. For what I want to do I do not do, but what I hate to do. 16 And if I do what I do not want to do, I agree that the law is good. 17 As it is, it is no longer I myself who do it, but it is sin living in me. 18 For I know that good itself does not dwell in me, that is in my sinful nature. For I have the desire to do what is good, but I cannot carry it out. 19 For I do not do the good I want to do, but the evil I do not want to do – this I keep on doing. 20 Now if I do what I do not want to do, it is no longer I who do it, but it is sin living in me that does it. 21 So I find this law at work: Although I want to do good, evil is right there with me. 22 For in my inner being I delight in God's law; 23 But I see another law at work on me, waging war against the law of my mind and making me a prisoner of the law of sin at work within me. 24 What a wretched man I am! Who will rescue me from this body that is subject to death? 25 Thanks be to God, who delivers me through Jesus Christ our Lord! So then, I myself in my mind am a slave to God's law, but in my sinful nature a slave to the law of sin." Romans 7:14-25 NIV

I mentioned in one of the earlier chapters that God is Love, and God is Good. All positive thoughts or attributes originate from God, such as Love, Honor, Joy, Peace, Happiness, Kindness, Forgiveness, etc. All of these are positive attributes, and we must follow them to be in sync with God.

By the same token, there are many negative thoughts or attributes that do not originate from God but from the Evil One, such as Hate, Envy, Theft, Murders, Adultery, etc. Any time we see ourselves following these negative attributes, we can be rest assured that we are not following the paths of Jesus or God. We are rather following the path of the Evil One.

It is very natural for us to commit wrong doings, because we are constantly under the influence of the Evil Force. We are always tempted to commit one, even though we know deep inside that it is wrong.

Every time we commit a sinful act or wrongdoing, we disregard God, and in its place we welcome the Evil One.

Also, many of us who accepted the Lord as our Savior feel that we can continue committing sins, because we accepted the Lord as our Savior and He forgave our sins. By accepting the Lord as our Savior does not automatically give us the green light to continue the path of further wrong doings. We must not take it for granted that He will continue to forgive us every time we repeat the same mistakes. We must remember that committing the wrong doings are all negative acts, and they originate from the Evil One. Every time we commit one we fall into the traps of the Evil One.

Let's take a look at some of the wrong doings that are very common among us. As a matter of fact, many of us think that they are ok in our society.

For example, the very first wrong doing by our very first ancestors was disobedience to God. Therefore, disobedience was sin. Actually, disobedience to God was the root of all evils.

How did that happen in the first place?

The Evil One had tempted our ancestors to commit the mistake.

What do we see in our society today? We see disobedience everywhere - children disobeying their parents; parents disobeying their elders; spouses disobeying spouses; students disobeying their teachers; teachers disobeying their school boards; employees disobeying their employers; employers disobeying the authorities; and so on. Many of us even believe that they are perfectly normal activities.

Let me ask a few questions.

Who tempted us to disobey in the first place? - The Evil One.

Who is behind all the disobediences today? Obviously, the very same one.

If the disobedience was not ok with God for the first time, why should it be ok with Him now?

There are many examples of wrong doings. We consider some as serious. Some are considered by us to be not so serious. But to God, let me assure you, however minor, all wrongdoings are not acceptable.

Let's take a look at a few more examples of wrong doings that are very common in our society today and were always present from the beginning.

Pride

Many of us take pride in our own achievements, whether it is success in our career, being rich, having luxuries, or whatever else that makes us proud. Whether we realize it or not, pride always becomes a barrier to our relationship with God.

Pride brings in us a false ego that we are smarter or better than others. Pride teaches us to be self-centered. It teaches us to serve ourselves. It becomes a barrier to our relationship with God, because pride originates from evil.

As a result, pride leads to broken relationships with others. It prevents us from loving and caring about others around us. Instead of thinking about what we can do to help and serve others, we, as prideful individuals, think only about how we can benefit from a relationship.

There is a saying in English, "Pride has its downfall." It is true. We can look in the history books. Whether it is about a specific person or a nation, a proud man or a proud nation always came down to its knees.

Why does Pride have its downfall? – Because pride causes us to emphasize ourselves more than God.

We begin to view ourselves as being important. It is not acceptable to God as pride originates from the Evil Force.

Greed

Greed also works hand-in-hand to make us proud. Greed is nothing but the excessive desire to have money, status, or power.

Having a moderate amount of wealth, status, or power is not a bad thing. But, when we become obsessed with earning more money, having more material things, status, and control, then we become too greedy.

Why do we become too greedy?

We know that possessions of certain things can bring us pleasure, and pleasure can be addictive. Pleasure and happiness are not the same attributes. But often we associate pleasure with happiness and, therefore, we pursue it without end.

Another reason for greed is fear. We are afraid there are only so many material things to go around, and, if we're not fast enough, someone else may take them before we can.

Although fear can cause greed, ironically greed causes more fear.

He who considers wealth a good thing can never bear to give up his income. He who considers eminence a good thing can never bear to give up his fame. He who has a taste for power can never bear to hand over authority to others.

When our desires become endless, we are serving the Evil One, not God.

Jealousy

Jealousy is an emotion. It typically comes from negative thoughts and feelings of insecurity, fear, and anxiety over an anticipated loss of something that the person values, such as a relationship, friendship, or love.

Jealousy often consists of a combination of emotions, such as anger, sadness, and disgust. Almost all human beings, at some point in their lives, become jealous of others over something.

That means we are envious of someone who has something we do not have. Being jealous indicates that we are not satisfied with what God has given us.

However, we need to be content with what we have. We need to remember that, when we serve God, He will give us the love, joy, peace, kindness, and self-control.

Jealousy originates from the negative force, the Evil One.

Laziness

Laziness comes from the negative force. It is often associated with depression and feeling low.

Sometimes it may come from the fear of failure. It often brings with it low self-esteem. When we have no confidence as to whether or not we will be successful in our endeavor, the negative force will tempt us to think that it is better not to try. We will have a tendency to not do anything. There is a saying in English. "An idle brain is the devil's workshop." It is true.

Adultery & Fornication

Adultery is illicit intimate sexual relationship between one man and one woman whereby the adulterer (offender) is currently married.

Fornication is a sexual intercourse between two people whereby the fornicator (offender) is not married.

It is possible to have one person to be a fornicator while the other could be an adulterer.

God has graciously provided for the sexual desires of men and women to be satisfied only in marriage. And to engage in pre-marital or extra-marital sex before or outside of marriage is to sin in God's sight.

The sin of adultery and fornication is serious in God's sight. Unfortunately, this sin is like an epidemic today everywhere we look.

This is undoubtedly the number one reason for almost all marriage breakdowns.

Indifference to God

There are so many doctrines, religions, and denominations today that some people can become easily confused, and they do not know what to believe or whom to believe.

They will take the path of indifference to God. In their minds, that is the right approach to take.

But creating the confusion and keeping people away from God are also the tactics used by the Evil One.

The purpose of these tactics is to keep us away from God, because that is his objective. Being indifferent to God does not solve the problem for us. Rather, we become further manipulated by the Evil One.

Over-Indulgence

God has given us our body and the need for nourishment, whether it is for food, drink or air. If we are taking food, we must know when to stop. If we are having drinks, we must know when to stop.

We must not over eat or over drink, especially when we are consuming beverages or substances that can make us intoxicated. Our body is not given to us for the purpose of abuse.

Covetousness

Covetousness means to have a strong desire to have something or someone that belongs to another person. Many among us are guilty of this sin without knowing the implications that result from this sin. Covetousness goes hand in hand with greed. Often, it leads to other kinds of sins such as adultery, theft, murder, sexual immorality, impurity and idolatry.

In many parts of the world, accepting bribes is a pretty common thing. Those who accept bribes they are coveting and committing sin whether they realize it or not. They are probably forgetting that a covetous person always brings trouble to his/her family.

Covetousness is the root of all kinds of sins. We must not fall into the temptations. In Luke 12:15, Jesus said, *"Watch out! Be on your guard against all kinds of greed; life does not consist in an abundance of possessions." - NIV*

There are many other types of sins, such as hatred, theft, false accusation, swearing, cursing, corruption, addiction, murdering, idolatry, etc.

We must remember that any action that originates from negative force is a wrong doing or sin. The only way we can overcome any of these temptations is by Divine intervention. What I mean by this is to focus on Jesus Christ. We cannot fight the evil alone by ourselves without the power of Christ.

Hebrews 2:18 says, *"Because he himself suffered when he was tempted, he is able to help those who are being tempted."* **Hebrews 2:18 NIV**

Every time we are tempted to commit a sin, let us make a commitment to call upon Jesus to guide us, and the Holy Spirit will come and rescue us without fail. We cannot fight the temptations on our own. We are not strong enough. We need the intervention by the Holy Spirit to keep us protected from the hands of Evil. Therefore, it is very important that we abide in Jesus all the time, otherwise, we cannot win.

Surrender Yourself Completely Unto Me in Your Daily Lives!

This is His third instruction for me and also for everyone, regardless of one's religion or background.

It is not easy for us to surrender completely. It is rather difficult.

In our world, surrendering to someone is almost like accepting our defeat.

With our ego, it is unthinkable. From our childhood, we have been taught to fight all the way to the end and never give in. We are always expected to win. Surrendering to someone almost sounds like a negative attribute to many of us.

What does "Surrender yourself completely to God" mean?

"Surrender myself completely to God" means to me that I yield, I submit, I obey, because I'm not here to win, overcome, or conquer Him. Rather, I'm here to surrender to His will.

I also know that God is not a cruel Master. He does not want to use His mighty force for us to surrender. He wants us to surrender to Him freely on our own.

Why do we need to surrender to Him? - Because we are like small children. We do not know what we do. We become very easily the victims of the Evil Force. We cannot overcome the evil temptations in our daily life unless we surrender to Him completely.

He wants us to surrender to Him completely because He loves us, and He is our Supreme Father. By surrendering to Him, we will discover that it brings us total freedom and immense joy, not bondage and sorrows.

As I mentioned earlier, our ego is the biggest culprit in our daily life. We take pride in everything we do or own.

What is the reason? Because we think we possess it. We have a big house, so we are proud! We have a big fancy car, so we are proud! We have a highly paid job, so we are proud! We have lots of money, so we are rich, and we are proud! We have a nice family, so we are proud!

We always think that we earned it, and we did it in our own way. We worked hard for them, therefore, we deserve them.

We believe whatever we possess is truly ours. The more we have, the more we want. Our ego never sleeps. It is always awake. It becomes a stumbling obstacle between us and God in our daily life.

We fall in love with our earthly possessions. We strongly believe whatever we have is ours and belongs to us forever. Our ego makes us believe that our earthly possessions are more important than God in our life.

If we could try a little harder to surrender ourselves completely to Him in our daily life, we would discover that everything we have in our daily life is really not ours.

Everything that we possess in this world actually belongs to Him, whether it is our family, our home, our car, our work, our friends, our life, and everything else that we really believe is ours.

They are not our property to begin with, and they will not remain to be our property.

Yet we are spending our entire life with our various emotions just to have control over them.

By surrendering completely to Him in our daily life, we acknowledge the fact that what we think we own is actually His property, not ours.

At the same time, we need to trust in Him that all our needs will be taken care of.

He is the giver of all positive things and, as long as they are given to us, our duty is to take care of them in good faith.

He is ultimately in control of everything, including our present circumstances.

Surrender yourself completely to God in our daily life means also giving each day to Him and let Him handle all of our worries, since He is in charge of our lives.

If we can surrender completely to Him in our daily life, we will be able to see that everything we always worked so hard for does not belong to us at all. They are all temporarily given to us for us to enjoy, but we must never forget that they can be easily taken away.

Most of us try to control our daily lives as if they are ours. If we have a good home, car, job, wealth, or whatever it is we love, and then it is taken away from us, what do we do? We always put the blame on God, who actually is the real owner of everything.

Is it fair? I do not think so. I think it is time for us to change.

Once we accept His Holy Spirit within ourselves, we must not be tempted to commit any such acts that will jeopardize our relationship with God.

But we are humans. We are bound to make some mistakes and commit some negative acts.

In the event we do such negative acts, we must confess our wrong doings to Him immediately and ask for His forgiveness.

We must ask for help from His Holy Spirit to give us the strength and wisdom to overpower the temptation, so that we do not commit the same mistake again.

Our life is a continuous journey to mature our relationship with Him. The objective is to grow.

We must not remain stagnant just because we say we believe in Him and He died for us. We must learn how to surrender ourselves completely to Him in our daily lives.

It is not an easy task, but we must demonstrate that we are honestly trying, not by saying alone, but through our actions. We will find that the more we surrender to God, the more we will resemble to Jesus. The objective in surrendering completely to God is for us to be like Jesus, always obedient to His Father. He always relied on His Father. He always knew the Father was in control, and, if we say that we are in Christ it means we are new creations, the old has gone, the new is here. God expects that we surrender everything to Him totally, not partially as it states in Romans 6:13.

"Do not offer any part of yourself to sin as an instrument of wickedness, but rather offer yourselves to God as those who have been brought from death to life; and offer every part of yourself to him as an instrument of righteousness." Romans 6:13 - NIV

Meditation & Prayers

Some people get defensive when they hear the word Meditation. Perhaps, in their mind, it triggers that we are not supposed to do meditation or they do not understand. They think that it originated from an Eastern culture. Therefore, it is not good for us to meditate. However, I'm not talking about TM or Transcendental Meditation, which originated from Eastern culture. I'm talking about Biblical Meditation.

In Joshua 1:8 God says to Joshua, *"Keep this Book of the Law always on your Lips; meditate on it day and night, so that you may be careful to do everything written in it. Then you will be prosperous and successful."- NIV*

We can see similar reference in Psalms 1:2 *"but whose delight is in the law of the Lord, and he who meditates on his law day and night." – NIV*

Meditation on God's Word and His Commandments is an important task for all people who claim to be born again. Being born again is the same as spiritual birth. When that happens, it opens our eyes to a deep understanding of Who God is and can become within us.

The spirit of God is inside everyone who is born again and only through Him can we experience true joy.

Biblical meditation opens up the Scriptures to us that causes us to grow in our understanding and relationship with God

When we meditate in the presence of God, the general tone of our thoughts and feelings gradually becomes lighter, more optimistic, more loving. Eventually, every area of our life will begin to reflect the sweet qualities of His Presence.

If we do not meditate, then we are missing the opportunity to come to the presence of our Savior, who is God Himself and who can turn every bit of our life to be full of positive qualities.

If our life is full of agony, we can easily turn that into a life full of peace and harmony. Therefore, "Surrender yourself completely to Him and then start meditating upon Him through the Scriptures."

However, we must be true and sincere in our efforts without hesitation and without fail. Once we are true and sincere with ourselves, it becomes very natural for us to be honest with God.

That does not mean we are going to be perfect all of the time, and we are not going to commit any more wrong doings.

Knowingly or unknowingly, we are bound to make some mistakes here and there. After all, we are human beings, and we are always being tempted by the evil force to commit one.

However, there will be a distinctive difference in us. The difference is: We will know as soon as we commit a mistake.

With the help of His Holy Spirit, we will instantaneously realize that we have committed a mistake. As soon as we realize our mistake, we must communicate our mistake with God and beg Him for His forgiveness.

How do we communicate with Him? We can communicate with Him either through meditation or through prayer.

Prayer is a way to communicate directly with Him. Prayer means talking directly to God and, when we pray, we must be sincere and genuine.

We must remember that God is our best friend, and we can talk to Him any time we want, 24 hours a day, 7 days a week, year-round. We do not have to be afraid to speak to Him, nor do we need to make an appointment to speak to Him.

By the same token, we do not need any special permission from anyone, including authorities or religious groups, when we want to talk to Him. It is all between us and Him.

We can talk to Him and share our thoughts, our feelings, our emotions and our concerns. He listens to all our prayers.

When we choose to combine prayer and meditation, it becomes a deep communion with God.

We must always begin with acknowledging and affirming His Presence. Then we must make a conscious movement in our heart to surrender our will to His Will. After re-aligning ourselves with God, we may meditate on our request.

However, it is important that we meditate from a position of faith, believing that God has heard our prayer, knowing He is in control, and as if our request has already been granted, while immersing our heart in a deep emotion of gratitude and love. If we meditate from a position of faith, our request will immediately begin to take form. It may take some time before we can see the result, but we must have faith that it is already in process.

There should be no doubts and fears. Doubts and fears are negative feelings.

When we pray and meditate, we must always do it from positive points of view. We must meditate on faith, strength, and patience, and, above all, we must guard our heart against fear.

God keeps all his promises. It is a growing-up process for us, as we want to build up our relationship with Him. Our objective should be not only to grow a relationship with Him but also to achieve a level of intimacy.

Therefore, it is necessary for us to communicate with Him on a regular basis, as often as we can. However, every time we meditate and pray, we should try to go just a little bit deeper than before. We can develop intensity without pressure and make an unforced effort.

We will soon realize that moving deep within toward the presence of God is the complete opposite of strain. Rather, it is conscious surrender and letting His Presence take over the experience.

At the end of our prayer and meditation, we must always release any attachment to the outcome.

It may not be easy at first, but we must develop complete trust in God and make this statement of faith every time we pray - "Your will be done on earth as it is in Heaven. Give us Peace, Lord!"

Is there any good time to talk to Him? - Some people think that early morning before sunrise is the most ideal time for meditation and prayers. But, for most of us, we are not even awake at that hour.

Therefore, it does not matter when we want to talk to Him and about what we want to talk to Him.

Practically, we can talk to Him just about any time when we are happy or when we are not so happy. We can talk to Him about how we feel, whether we are upset about something, or whether we failed to do something right. He wants to hear from us as naturally as we would speak to our closest friend.

However, for effective communications, we should find a quiet place and a quiet time where we will be undistracted.

We must have concentration of mind and, as we are speaking to Him, we cannot have our mind travel in many different directions. It is essential that we practice to be calm and quiet.

We should not attempt meditation until we have calmed down all mental and emotional attachments. But we should do our prayers.

We should never take our worries and fears into a meditative state. In that case, they will be amplified, which, in turn, will send a strong instruction to our subconscious mind. If we were completely free from all fears and our faith were strong and deep, the outcome will always be good because God is good.

Communications are always two-way channels. If one speaks all the time and the other one only listens, then it is not a good communication.

It is no different when we talk to God. We must not talk all the time. After we pray or talk to Him, we must have a period of silence, so we can hear His voice as He speaks to us.

Through the meditation and positive thoughts, we will know when He grants our prayers. However, we must be careful of what we pray for and how we pray.

God is not going to grant us everything that we ask. If we are going to ask for something in order to gain our personal wealth, status, or career, that is going to be viewed by Him as a barrier in our personal relationship with Him.

We can be rest-assured that our prayers will not be answered. We must know the difference between need and want. He knows our needs, and He will definitely take care of them. That does not mean He will give us everything we want.

It is also common for us to pray for ourselves and for our loved ones. There is nothing wrong with that.

But, as we want to grow our relationship with Him, we must learn how to pray for others. God is pleased when we sincerely pray for others. This shows that we are not self-centered, but we are compassionate.

In order to have a long-lasting relationship with Him, we must let go of our ego.

When we are out of touch with the indwelling Spirit most of our conscious time, we allow our ego to run our life. Our ego is never asleep and is always ready to fight for its territory at a moment's notice.

Our ego stands between our soul and God. It will never let God enter unless we tame it by regular prayer and meditation. If we fail to control our own ego, chances are the evil one will take control of our ego and use that to keep us away from God.

While meditating or praying, we must empty our mind of negativity and let God fill it with love, wisdom, and bliss. We should simply be a channel for God's will.

Therefore, let's keep on meditating and praying as often as we can.

We need to be in sync with Him while we are still alive.

A corpse has every organ, bone, and body system that we have. The only difference between us and the corpse is the spark of life that we enjoy. This is our real self and is eternal and infinite. The real self is part of Him, because it is He Who has breathed life into us.

Every time our meditations and prayers are answered, we must not forget to communicate with Him by saying, "Thank you, Lord! Thank you for answering my prayers."

We must not forget that everything we have is a gift of love from Him.

Walk With Me

This was His fourth instruction to me. For quite some time I was not sure what He meant by this instruction. How can I walk with God? I am 5'6" tall, and He appeared to me as a Giant about 70' tall. His one step will be many times larger than mine. When He walks I definitely have to run very fast just to keep up with His single pace. This certainly didn't appeal to me to be a normal walk when one walks at a steady pace and the other person has to run a race to catch up with his single pace. Also, I never heard this terminology in my limited exposure of my previous background. I knew there had to be a different interpretation for its meaning, but I didn't know where to find the true answer.

Not knowing where to start I decided to look onto the Ten Commandments established by God Himself through Moses for the Israelites. I believed that I had to obey the Ten Commandments for me to be able to walk with Him.

Let's take a look at them. However, I realize that many of my Readers are probably not familiar with the Ten Commandments, so I think it will be appropriate for me to quote them from the Bible at this time. For the Readers who are not familiar with the Bible, The Ten Commandments can be found in two different places in the Bible, first in Exodus 20:2-17 and then in Deuteronomy 5:6-21. They are both identical with very minor differences in some words. For the benefit of my Readers, I'm quoting a summarized version of them.

The Ten Commandments
1. You shall have no other gods before Me.
2. You shall not make any idols (You shall not make for yourself a carved image – any likeness of anything that is in heaven above, or that is in earth beneath, or that is in the water under the earth; you shall not bow down to them nor serve them.)

3. You shall not take the name of the Lord your God in vain.
4. Remember the Sabbath day, to keep it holy. (Six days you shall labor and do all your work, but the seventh day is the Sabbath of the lord your God. In it you shall do no work.)
5. Honor your father and your mother.
6. You shall not murder.
7. You shall not commit adultery.
8. You shall not steal.
9. You shall not bear false witness against your neighbor.
10. You shall not covet anything that is your neighbor's.

After reading and understanding the Ten Commandments, I wanted to see where I stand personally in my situation. I found that I was ok from the third commandment to the tenth. As a matter of fact, my parents were very strict in following them, simply as Family Rules.

But I realized that I was in deep trouble with the first and the second commandments. Since I was born and raised in a culture that practiced worshipping many gods, I did the same. I didn't know anything different. All my ancestors did it, so why shouldn't I? If I failed to do so, I'd be condemned by my family, as well as the community. I'm certain there might be some repercussions that would have followed.

This is a prime example of how a child gets automatically influenced by the society or the environment he/she is born into. It is a standard practice everywhere.

Not only did I worship many idols that were carved images, but they were in the likeness of various things in heaven above, or earth beneath, or water under the earth. I worshipped, bowed down to them, and served them without any hesitation. I never thought for a single moment that this would be a wrongful practice for me. Millions of people still do them on a regular basis, and they think the same way.

Who am I to tell others what to do and not to do? This is not up to me. It is entirely up to each individual to make that decision whom they will worship and how they will worship. God has given us a free will so that each one of us can make that decision on our own.

The only thing I can speak about is me. Undoubtedly, I would have continued to do what I used to do, if I did not have the Divine Encounter.

That unexpected encounter I had with the Lord changed me forever. Since then, His Holy Spirit has been guiding me daily on what I should do or I should not do. Now it is unthinkable for me to disregard any of God's Commandments. I would not dare to break His Law. I know the consequences will not be good for me or anyone else.

I was definitely guilty of breaking the first two commandments. But the second commandment about not worshipping any idols is a much bigger issue today.

In Deuteronomy 4:28 God is saying: *"There you will worship man-made gods of wood and stone, which cannot see or hear or eat or smell." –NIV*

Idol worshipping displeases God very much. When we worship an idol, considering the image as a superior power or force, we are committing a grave offence whether we are aware of it or not.

Idol worshipping does not mean the worshipping of a statue as a specific shape or form only. Idol can be anything other than God Himself whom we worship.

Let me give a few examples of idol worshipping that are very common to people from all backgrounds and religions today.

Over-indulgence or falling in love with money, career, power, lust, addiction, wealth or attraction to any other material possessions that bring false pride into us are considered to be idol worshipping.

How many people do we really know who can be excluded from the idol worshipping? It is not limited to certain religions or faiths. It is everywhere.

People from all faiths and backgrounds are guilty of this wrong doing. It does not matter of which socio-economic background we come from. We are all guilty of some sort of idol-worshipping, whether the idol is money, career, movie stars, super sport figures, stock market, wealth, or lust.

There are very few people who do not worship some types of idols, since the form of idols may vary from place to place or from generation to generation.

It does not matter what types of idols we like to worship. The principle of idol worshipping remains the same - worshipping something else other than God.

It can take different forms from region to region.

Today it is a known fact that all over the world almost everyone is in love with some sort of new high-tech gadget, i.e., video games, iPhones, Internet, Facebook, and other social media, cell phones or anything else that can keep us entertained or occupied for hours and days. Most people also find them inseparable for their survival today.

There is no doubt that our focus today has shifted to new types of idols. If we are not worshipping new high-tech gadgets, then we may find ourselves worshipping the money market to the point that our personal emotions get intimately involved with the gain or loss of the wealth.

The reality is – most everyone is worshipping some sort of idols, knowingly or unknowingly. And most of us think that's perfectly ok, since we are bettering ourselves and not harming others. And, if for some reason we cannot indulge in the vastly popular or common types of idol worshipping, we can always worship one in the name of our religion.

There are endless examples of idol worshipping, but the most common one throughout the world is money.

Jesus said in Matthew 6:24, ***"No one can serve two masters. Either you will hate one and love the other, or you will be devoted to one and despise the other. You cannot serve both God and money." – NIV***

In order to walk with God, our hearts must be in sync with God. In order to be in sync with God our hearts must be true, sincere and honest with God always. God never says not to use any of the materialistic things. It is ok to use any of these gadgets as we need them. But, whenever we have over-indulgence or obsessions with any materialistic thing, that object then becomes an idol for us. If that happens, we become the idol worshippers. An idol worshipper cannot walk with God.

Walking with God also means walking in the same direction as God wants to go.

Whenever two of us walk together, both of us must walk in the same direction. If one walks forward and the other one walks to the opposite direction, then we are not walking with each other. We are more or less walking on our own.

How do we know if we are walking with God? Anyone who is walking with God knows the direction God moves. God is the originator of all positive attributes. Therefore, if we are full of positive behavior, as well as positive actions, we are walking with Him.

The moment we are under the negative influence, we are committing wrong doings or sins. In that instance, God and we are walking at 180 degrees apart from each other. In other words, we are not walking with Him - we are walking on our own.

When God created the first man and the first woman, it was His intention that they would walk with Him on a regular basis. We know that His intention did not last long, because of our ancestors' disobedience to Him. Disobedience caused them and God to walk at 180 degrees apart.

The lesson learned from this should be that we must remain obedient to God at all times. In order to be able to walk with Him, first we must offer a sincere apology to God for our wrongful behavior, and then we must remain obedient to Him.

We cannot walk with God if we are proud of ourselves, whether we are proud of our wealth, status, job, or any other achievements.

Whenever we become proud of any of our achievements, we automatically become self-centered. We do not become God–centered, nor do we become dependent on Him. We become self- dependent. God cannot walk with any such person. In order to walk with Him, we must humble ourselves.

Also, when we walk with someone, both persons must walk at the same pace in order to walk together. If one person moves ahead or falls behind, then they are not walking together. Similarly, when we walk with Him, we cannot get ahead of Him or fall behind Him. We must keep our pace together with Him.

Also, we cannot stand still. Then, it is not a walk.

Unfortunately, many of us who accepted the Lord as our Savior would like to remain static.

Static also means doing nothing. Doing nothing is inaction and, therefore, we will remain still at the same place. But God does not stand still. He moves, and we must move at the same pace with Him, if we want to walk with Him.

Whenever we walk with our human father, we usually talk to each other and listen to each other. We share our thoughts, our feelings, and our emotions. This way we develop an intimate relationship.

The relationship can be intimate, but, at the same time, we respect our father, and we revere Him. God is our Eternal Father. When we walk with

Him, our relationship can be intimate, but, at the same time, we must have honor and respect for Him in our hearts.

It is important that we walk with God every day because walking with God can be very rewarding for us. Walking with God should be a part of our daily schedule.

If our day-to-day life gets to be such that we have time for everything but not for walking with God, then it is time for us to stop everything for a moment and take a deep breath. As we inhale the deep breath, we must be thankful to God that He gave us the privilege to take that deep breath.

We must not forget that the breath He gave us can be taken away from us without any warning or without any notice.

Nothing in this world can be more rewarding than to surrender to God and walk with Him.

Our life will not be happy and joyful, if we do not learn how to walk with God. Our personal life, our family, or any other responsibility will not be fully realized until we walk with God on a regular basis.

By the same token, we cannot be impatient for rewards when we walk with God.

Nobody says that it is going to be easy to walk with God. During our walk, if we happen to trip and fall, let's not get discouraged, because He is going to carry us when we are lying low.

In this context, I remember a beautiful note/poem, Footprints (author unknown/anonymous), that is worth mentioning here. It goes like this.

"One night I had a dream. I dreamed I was walking along the beach with God, and across the sky flashed the scenes from my life. For each scene, I noticed two sets of footprints on the sand. One belonged to me, the other to God. When the last scene of my life flashed before us, I looked back at the footprints in the sand. I noticed that many times along the path of life there was only one set of footprints. I also noticed that it happened at the very lowest and saddest times in my life. This really bothered me, and I questioned God about it. 'God, you said that once I decided to follow you, you would walk with me all the way, but I noticed that during the most troublesome time in my life there is only one set of footprints. I don't understand why in times when I needed you most you would leave me.' God replied, 'My precious, precious child, I love you, and I would never,

never leave you during your times of trials and suffering. When you see only one set of footprints, it was then that I carried you.'"

How beautiful and reassuring the note is! Let us keep our faith in Him. He is definitely going to carry us when we are unable to carry ourselves.

HEAVEN & HELL

Heaven and Hell are real. If anyone is skeptical about their existence, all I can say to them is that I have seen the beauty of the magnificent Heaven with my own eyes. At the same time, where I stood by the edge of a platform, I could also see down below the scary dark world we refer to as Hell.

The Heaven, as I saw it, is a large compound that was enclosed with very high and extraordinarily beautiful fences on all four sides. The area inside was the most beautiful large compound I had ever seen in my life. Nothing in this world could ever come close to the beauty of this place. The fences were tall, but they were magnificent. I was so taken by the beauty of the place inside that I could not keep my eyes away from it. The more I saw, the more curious I became, and I wanted to see more.

The brightness of the Light did not blind me any longer. Rather, it was shining upon the entire compound with a soothing light, similar to the moonlight on a full moon night, only several times brighter. Because of the soothing Light shining upon the area, I was able to see the entire huge compound very clearly.

I saw there were many marvelous big buildings after buildings. Big buildings would be an understatement. I should say there were mansions after mansions, and they were so gorgeous and beautiful.

The mansions were very large in size; their structures were superb; and their roofs were of a bright golden color. Some of the mansions also had bright copper colored roofs.

I've not seen anything like these mansions anywhere in the world. The beauty of this place was unique, unlike any other beautiful place I've ever seen. Its beauty was awesome and beyond description.

I could not turn my eyes away from this magnificent place. The more I saw, the more I was getting stunningly astonished. As soon as I saw this place, I fell in love with it. Instantly, I knew that this is my ultimate goal; this is the only objective of my life, to be inside this beautiful compound.

I also saw many angels there who were floating on the air. The arched fences had posts every 1000 feet or so apart. There was an angel on each of these posts. It appeared to me that the angels were protecting the boundary, keeping a watchful eye for an intruder. It was evident to me that the angels not only protect the area from undesirable intrusion, but they also manage the entire area to keep it always under total control.

The entire area is on top of a very high ground, and the tall fences are mounted on top of an abyss (very steep and extremely difficult to climb). At the center of this beautiful compound, where all the marvelous royal mansions were, the area appeared to me as a superbly planned city of golden colored roofs. Also inside the compound were beautiful gardens and park-like settings.

From the center of the compound, there were 12 different roads or pathways that went all the way to the outer walls. The paths are equally distributed, one at each corner and two additional per side. The entire area seemed to me to be a square shaped compound. At the end of each road by the wall there is a gateway to the Kingdom of Heaven. Therefore, there are 12 gates in heaven.

I wanted to go inside the fences. I was looking for an entrance through a gateway. I asked myself, "Where are the entranceways to this place?" I continually searched for an entranceway all around the perimeters as far as I could see, but I could not find one. The gates must have been completely sealed. I could not find a single entranceway to this beautiful place.

I was desperately searching for one. Not finding any entranceway made me sad. But, as I looked inside the fences, I knew there were no sadness, no grief, no pain, and no sorrows there. I knew once I entered there, it would be eternally peaceful with immense joy and happiness. No impure thing or person can exist there. It is undoubtedly the home of the righteous.

It is also the place with no darkness at all. There is always light in heaven. There is no such thing as night, as we know here on earth. The Divine Light whom I accompanied there stopped a little high above the compound and, from the brilliance of this Divine Light, the entire area was lit. The light did not feel too bright. Rather, it was a soothing light.

The walls and the fences appeared to be the color of pearls. Their brilliance was radiant.

There are a few things I noticed that are worth mentioning here. When we depart from the earth, our body stays behind, but our mind and spirit travel to the next destination. Also, I noticed that my vision there was completely different than the vision I have here. There, my vision had no limitations. I could see from one end of heaven to the other. I could also zoom in on any specific item and see every minute detail, similar to a microscope and telescope.

The other thing that was obvious to me was that the angels were the administrators in the Kingdom of Heaven. The angels were there to ensure that everything works flawlessly and perfectly.

I was standing at the far left corner of a platform from where I could easily fall off the edge just by trembling. Earlier, I looked down below where I would fall. Standing from the edge looking down below on my left what I had seen there was the most dreadful place.

The fall would drop me to a place that was many thousands of miles deep into the dark valley of death. I glimpsed at the most gruesome place, and the view was the most frightening one. There is no doubt in my mind that the place that I saw down below was the place of permanent death with no return. The place that I saw below was what we refer to as Hell.

How did the Hell look to me? I only saw the top view of Hell.

From where I saw, it was just the opposite of what I witnessed in Heaven. There was no darkness in Heaven; there was always light. It was just the opposite in Hell. There was no light in Hell; it was always dark. The only light that I could see was of burning flame.

Heaven was the place of joy, happiness, and love. The Hell was the place of sorrows, sadness, and hate. Undoubtedly, it was the place of torments and weeping forever. It was a place of unrest. I have no doubt in my mind that the Hell was a place of separation and a place completely shut out from the presence of God and His Mercy.

From where I was standing, I was able to witness the intense beauty of Heaven in front of my eyes. At the same time, I could look below on my left, where I could see the unknown scary world. It was so frightening that I immediately stepped a few feet away from the edge, fearing that I might fall. As a result, I spent most of my time desperately searching for an entranceway into the magnificent Kingdom of Heaven.

When I came face-to-Face with God, I saw His Face only once. I could not look at His Face for a second time, since I started to tremble vigorously with fear. The Lord appeared to me as a Giant. I knew He was not going to spare me, since I committed sins. I could not raise my head due to fear and guilt. I was continuously looking at His Feet.

As I looked towards His Feet and a few hundred feet on His left, I noticed a very Narrow Door that could take me inside the Heaven.

For what I had witnessed, this Narrow Door is the One and Only Entranceway into the Kingdom of Heaven.

The Lord was sitting there on a throne near to the door as if He was guarding that door.

The Lord is such a Giant, and I could not dare to go through the door, unless the Lord permitted me to enter.

Therefore, no one will dare to go through the narrow door unless the Lord lets one in. Now, I find the references of this narrow door in the Bible in two places.

In Matthew 7:13-14

13 "Enter through the narrow gate. For wide is the gate and broad is the road that leads to destruction, and many enter through it. 14 But small is the gate and narrow the road that leads to life, and only a few find it." – NIV

In Luke 13:24

"Make every effort to enter through the narrow door, because many, I tell you, will try to enter and will not be able to." - NIV

Follow Darkness or the Light?

A short time ago, I had an opportunity to speak to a very learned man. He was considered to be a very intelligent and honorable person in the community. It was my honor to have an opportunity to carry on spiritual discussions with a distinguished scholar.

During the conversation, I found that he was very dominating, as well as quite forceful, in his belief that we, the humans, were not created by God. He was very adamant that we humans evolved from apes. He was such a learned person that someone such as I would definitely hesitate to challenge his views and argue with him.

However, he didn't waste any time letting me know his view that there was no such being as God. Frankly speaking, I didn't see any point in arguing with him, as it was futile. Besides, he was such a well-known scholar, and anything I would say would be viewed by him as my ignorance.

Later, I kept wondering why is it that many highly educated people find it so difficult to accept the truth that we humans have been created by God. I kept wondering what would be the purpose of having a higher education.

I would think that the purpose of having a higher education is to increase our knowledge-base. After receiving a few degrees from a reputable institution, does our knowledge-based increase more than the knowledge of the eternal truth? Will we ever get to the point where our knowledge-base will ever be equal to or higher than our Creator? If that was the case, we would be immortal like our Creator after acquiring several higher degrees.

But it does not work that way. Truly speaking, it does not matter whether we are highly educated or quite uneducated. The truth is: we came to this world with nothing, and we would leave this world with nothing.

Absolutely nothing from this world will accompany us when it is time for us to depart.

To anyone who is even slightly doubtful of the existence of God, all I can emphasize from my personal experience is that we are not only created by God, but we are also created in His image. We can look all around us, and what we will find is that in all of His creation only we, the human beings, are made in God's image; no other creatures are.

This should be taken as a great honor for us, and it should give us dignity. We may not know exactly what "God's image" means, but we do know some of the aspects, which include:

- Like God, we are spiritual beings - our spirits are immortal and will outlast our earthly bodies.
- We are intellectual - we can think, reason, and solve problems.
- We are relational - we can give and receive real love.
- We have a moral conscious - we can discern right from wrong, which makes us accountable to God.

Do we see one other creature in the entire universe that is like us? We can take a good look all around us over and over again. We will repeatedly find that we humans are the one and only creatures. There is no other creation in the universe like us. We are very different from everything else.

Did we evolve just by accident, or did we evolve from the monkeys?

Nothing evolves from accidents; everything is predetermined. And to think that we evolved from the monkeys is to defame the human race. It does not make any sense at all. It probably would have made more sense if we were to say that monkeys evolved from men.

But then we would be very quick to protest. "That is absurd! How can monkeys come from men?" Why not? If the learned people truly believe that men came from monkeys, why can't the monkeys come from men? Why is it not possible?

The truth is: Monkeys can come only from monkeys. Men can come only from men. Life can only originate from life. We did not evolve on our own, by chance, or by accident.

Why is it so difficult to accept? And it seems that the more learned we are the more difficult it is for us to accept the Truth.

Whether we want to accept it or not, the Truth remains the same – we have been created by God in His image.

Unfortunately, the image is not complete and has been damaged. Our image had been distorted due to the temptation of the Evil Force from the beginning.

We must never underestimate the power of the Evil Force. The Evil Force is deceptive and quite powerful.

We know that the Evil Force lured us to commit disobedience to God. Actually, when we committed our very first disobedience, we did not know fully what we were doing at the time, because we were too vulnerable like our young children. We thought we knew everything, but we had no idea what we were doing.

Why did we do so?

We did so because we were tempted by the Evil Force to do exactly the opposite of what God instructed us to do. At the time, we did not know what we were doing. But the Evil One knew exactly what he was doing.

Consequently, we became victims of the circumstances, similar to a typical young child who gets lured away by an evil kidnapper with distorted motives. The child who becomes the victim of the circumstances may think he/she knows what the evil kidnapper is doing. But, honestly speaking, does the child really know that he/she became a victim? Does the child really know what is going to happen to him/her?

Whenever a young child is kidnapped by an evil doer, the child becomes separated from his/her loving home and loving parents. If the child continues to live in his/her new environment, he/she will do exactly what the evil doers are doing, The child does not know differently, and the new environment will be his/her norm.

Our situation is quite similar. Since the day we were separated from God, we have been under the influence of the Evil Force who is continuously tempting us to commit more and more wrong doings. There is only one motivation that the Evil One has, and that is to destroy us forever. He knows very well that the more wrong doings we commit, the further we will move away from God.

With my personal encounter with God, I can assure you that God did not create us to be away from Him. The purpose of His creating us in His image was to be like Him. He wanted us to be eternally with Him as His family, His friend, His trustworthy companion.

The problem for us is that God is pure, but we are not. In order for us to be with Him and to stay with Him, we must be pure. Our thoughts and actions must remain pure not sometime, not whenever we intend, but all the time.

Purity can be obtained only from our continual walk with God and reliance on His leading, the Positive Divine Force. In order to be blessed with purity, there is absolutely no room for any negative thoughts, ideas, behavior, or attitude, because they originate from the evil or negative force.

Let us take a good look at ourselves and have an honest evaluation of our own nature. What do we see within us? Are we honest? Are we sincere? Are we truthful? Are we pure, if not all the time, most of the time?

How many people can we find in the entire world who can truly say, "God, I have been absolutely honest throughout my life? I have never told any lies. I have never committed any sins of any type. I have never been envious or jealous of another person. I have never cheated or taken someone else's belongings. I have never looked at another person with lust. I have never been greedy, etc., etc."

Let us be honest. How many people can raise their hands and say they fit that description? Chances are there are none.

Yet most of us think of ourselves as being ok; there is nothing wrong with us. But we know better of ourselves. And it is most likely a truer statement if we say, "Each and every one of us is guilty of some wrong doing." In the eyes of God, just one wrong doing is sufficient to lose the definition of purity.

Committing wrong doings has been engrained into our character from the day we lost our real home, just like the young child who has been growing up in the company of the evil kidnapper. As a matter of fact, committing wrong doings has become a norm for us. It has become so common today in our society. Even if we could find one single individual who would be relatively truthful or honest, most people would find that individual to be strange and, to some extent, weird because that person is out of the "norm."

In today's world, most people think it is ok to tell lies, even if their conscience tells them it is not. Most people are self-centered and treat themselves as their number one priority. Many people are out to cheat their own brothers, friends, and family members, which includes people from all religions and faiths. There is no exception.

What do we think - God is pleased with us?

We can be all His children. What would be our reaction as parents if we find that our own children are doing everything that they are not supposed to do?

Wouldn't our normal reaction be full of anger and shock?

I would think that most parents would consider some type of disciplinary action in order to correct the undesired behavior of their children.

How would the parents feel when they found out their loving children have not rectified their mistakes, despite repeated warnings? And, to the contrary, they are committing more severe acts that are unacceptable to the parents?

I would think that would make any loving parents furious.

What about God?

He is our loving Father. How does He feel when He sees us doing everything that we are not supposed to do, including worshipping idols?

There are endless examples of idol worshipping, but the most common one throughout the world is money.

Jesus said to his disciples, *23 "Truly I tell you, it is hard for someone who is rich to enter the kingdom of heaven. 24 Again I tell you, it is easier for a camel to go through the eye of a needle than for someone who is rich to enter the kingdom of God." Matthew 19:23-24 - NIV*

Is money the root of all evils? Certainly, Jesus is not saying that making money is evil. It is perfectly ok to make money by honest means and not by cheating others. In today's world, it is absolutely necessary for us to survive. There is nothing wrong in doing that. He knows that.

But what is wrong is falling in love with the money - especially, the rich people with lots of money. It is never enough. They want more and more. They become greedy. They are never satisfied. They feel that money brings them a sense of security, and false pride gets into them.

We tend to measure everything and everyone by the amount of money we possess in relationship to one another. We strongly believe that if someone has much money then he/she can do anything, and the one who has very little is considered to be very poor. Our society treats people with money differently than the people with no money. This is true everywhere.

As people with money become addicted to making more and more, they start thinking that money is mightier than anything else. Making more money becomes the primary objective, and everything else becomes secondary or less important. A false sense of security sets in.

They tend to forget the real purpose of their life. A false sense of security and pride will lead them to their spiritual destruction. They tend to forget that the money they possess is not their own. It does not belong to them permanently. Someone else had that money before them, and someone else will have it afterwards.

Money never stays permanently with anyone. It was given to the current owners for a temporary period of time. It can be taken away from them in the blink of an eye, with one blow, and then all of a sudden the money of which they were so proud is worth nothing.

Even the rich men that Jesus mentioned can find their salvation through Him. But they need to change their attitude and behavior. They need to make up their mind whether they are going to serve money or God and act accordingly. Jesus said we cannot have two Masters.

Jesus confirmed by saying to His disciples, ***"With man this is impossible, but with God all things are possible." Matthew19:26 – NIV.*** That indicates that we have a loving God who can forgive and make it possible for the rich men to be with God provided they change themselves.

In this world, just to have a little more money many among us are committing many negative acts. What is the reason? We are continuously being tempted by the Evil Force to commit more and more wrong doings. The Evil Force knows the more we commit wrong doings, the further we'll get away from God.

How are we tempted? If we take a step back and look at it deeper, we will find that almost all of our temptations come through our thoughts.

Temptation begins by capturing our attention. What gets our attention arouses our emotions. Then our emotions activate our behavior, and we act on what we feel. The more we think about something, the stronger it takes hold of us, and that is why we should refrain from anything that gives us the evil thoughts.

We should stay close to anything that motivates us to do right. How do we know what is right or what is wrong?

Any actions that give us true peace, happiness, and joy are right thoughts. All right thoughts come from the Divine source that is full of love. Similarly, any actions that give us shame, sadness, false pride, and make our life miserable are wrongful thoughts and come from the evil one.

We should know that a lot of wrongful thoughts come in the form of temptation. It is up to us to decide whether we accept or reject the temptation. Most often we do not even know the differences between the two, and, therefore, we fall victims to the temptation. But the consequences of each temptation drift us further away from the Divine One.

How can we avoid becoming a victim of the temptation?

Some people think that ignoring a temptation is far more effective than fighting it. Once our mind is on something else, the temptation loses its power. But, realistically, are we stronger than the Evil One? Let us not fool ourselves. The Evil One is far more powerful than we are. We are no match for him. Otherwise, we would not have fallen victims in the first place. The Evil One is far more powerful than we are, but not mightier than our Lord.

Sometimes it may appear that the Evil Force is winning, but, in the end, we know that God has overcome the evil one. There should be no doubt that the Living God is far mightier than the negative force or the evil one.

We can see throughout the history of all nations that Truth always won in the end, and Truth will always win in the future. This should act as a convincing reminder to all of us that whenever we are tempted, we should not deviate from the Truth.

Can we fight the temptations of the Evil One by ourselves, and how can we win?

We simply cannot do it by ourselves. In order to fight the temptations of the Evil One, we definitely must seek help from God.

Spiritually, our mind is our most vulnerable organ. To reduce temptation, we must keep our mind occupied with positive influences and other good thoughts. We can defeat negative thoughts by thinking of something more positive. This is the principle of replacement.

The choice is ours. We are created with our own free will. If we have the will to defeat the negative temptations, we certainly can overcome evil with good. In order to defeat the negative temptations, we will need the help from the Spirit of God.

All we need to do is to invite Jesus to come into our hearts and into our lives. If we can get the support of Jesus, only then can we overcome the enemy because Jesus defeated the Evil by His own blood shed.

Our situation in this world is similar to the kidnapped child by the evil person with distorted motive. How can a kidnapped young child free himself/herself from the captivity of the evil doer unless a higher authority intervenes? It is simply not possible.

There is a saying that "an idle mind is the devil's workshop." It is absolutely true. At the same time, it is also true that the Evil Force cannot get our attention when our mind is preoccupied with something else that is Positive. That's why we need to keep our minds focused. We must fix our thoughts on Jesus. We must keep our minds fixed on those things that are good, things that are true, noble, right, pure, lovely, and honorable. *"Finally, brothers and sisters, whatever is true, whatever is noble, whatever is right, whatever is pure, whatever is lovely, whatever is admirable – if anything is excellent or praiseworthy – think about such things." Philippian 4:8 - NIV*

If we are serious about defeating temptation, we must be able to manage our mind. With the help from the Holy Spirit, we can filter out the negative thoughts. We should pay attention to how we think, because our life is shaped by our thoughts. Our thoughts are influenced by our daily life, environments, and surroundings.

Generally speaking, we accept what the majority of others are doing. If it is ok what most others do, then why shouldn't it be ok for us? If most others are not telling the truth, and it is ok for them, then why should not that be ok for us? If the majority of people are spending much of their time in idol-worshipping and they are causing no harm to anyone, why shouldn't that be ok for us?

Our thoughts must not be influenced by what the majority of others are doing. The majority of others are not following the path of the Jesus Christ.

Let us not forget that God created us with our own free will. He gave us the intellects and the wisdom for us to think and analyze, to rationalize what is right and what is wrong. It seems that the average person is not even applying this amazing power that we inherited from God.

Today, as an average person, we do not have any time to think, and we are so busy doing our own things. We are very busy fighting for our own survival. Truly speaking, from the day we are born into this world until the time of our death, our life is full of fighting continuous battles of one type or another.

The battle for survival is only one example of our life. The battles that we face in this world can take many different forms. We are all running rat races in our day-to-day survival games.

Millions of people are without jobs. Unless we are in their shoes, we have no idea how difficult it is to make ends meet. What would be the priorities for the people with no jobs and no earnings? As far as they are concerned, the day-to-day survival is the most important goal for them. Why would they spend any time to come to God and surrender to Him? If they did, they would be considered by others as strange people.

Then we have wars between nations. We all know how difficult it is to survive when two nations go to fight wars. Many lives are lost. Both nations want to win. Nobody wants to surrender. But we know the Truth will always triumph in the end at the cost of the many lost lives.

Similarly, we will find that there are all kinds of battles going on between the people of different colors, races, ethnic origins, religions, cultures, languages, etc., etc. The battles can also be between two opposite sexes; between the rich people and the poor; or among various members in one family. There are no shortages of battles in this world. All of these battles in our life are only to distract us from our original selves.

But the biggest battle we will fight in our life is within ourselves. Everyone will face this battle sooner or later. It is the battle among the good and the evil, representing within us our battles against our flesh. Whether we decide to follow after the things of God or not, is entirely up to us.

The path of falling into the temptations of this world is very easy, and most of the time we are not even aware of it as we fall victims to these temptations. However, we can follow after Christ with the power of the Holy Spirit.

We must not forget that the consequences of following after the things of the world will lead only to death. Following after God will lead to eternal peace, joy, and happiness. The choice is ours, and we will need to make that decision before our life ends here on earth. The sooner we can come to conclusion, the better it is for us.

Whenever things do not go in the same direction we anticipate, we always try to blame it on God. We fail to recognize that, in most cases, the consequences resulted from the actions or inactions of our own. But that does not stop us. We are always quick to blame it on God. We are also not aware of the fact that many battles in our life are due to the temptations of the Evil Force only to keep our thoughts occupied with negative attributes. The less time we can have to think about the things of God is better for the evil one. He appears to win as he takes control of that life towards darkness.

From my own experience with God, I can reassure you that He did not send us to the earth to remain in the darkness throughout our lives. The purpose of this life is to discover our real selves, who we really are, and understand that we are all part of Him. We all can be His children.

Since He created us in the first place to be with Him forever, that's what He wants. We had been separated from Him. But He still loves each and every one of us, and He wants every one of us back to Him. He also knows that our wrong doings are not getting any less. Rather, we are committing more and more every day and, as a result, we are drifting further away from Him.

But it is true that the majority of us want to live a peaceful and harmonious life. Some people are fortunate to have the peace and harmony in their life. For others, it does not appear to happen, despite making our best efforts. Sometimes we wonder why is it that peaceful existence does not take place, whether it is between two people or between two members of the same family. If we could live here on earth peacefully, then there would be no issue. The problem is that, even if we try to live peacefully, there would be no permanent peace.

Why is it that way? Why can we not live peacefully? Is it possible for us to live a peaceful life?

Yes, it is possible. The only way we can live in peace is if we are walking with God.

Otherwise, there will be no peace for us, because He did not send us to live a comfortable and peaceful life on earth while we had been worshipping some sort of idols and turning our backs on Him. It does not work that way.

This life was given for us to wake up as if we are in a deep sleep. We must be born again. Each and every one of us must have a second birth. The second birth does not mean reincarnation. The second birth means to be born spiritually.

Jesus replied to Nicodemus, *"Very truly I tell you, no one can see the kingdom of God unless they are born again." John 3:3 – NIV*

Unless we are born the second time of the spiritual birth, we will not be able to be in harmony with God.

Without having the powerful influence of the Holy Spirt, we cannot achieve peace or happiness. By default, we are born unto sin through the sin of Adam. The only way we can overcome the enemy is through Jesus Christ, our Savior.

This is the key factor for us to be in right standing with God, our Creator. It is difficult for us to have a spiritual birth because society, environment, and surroundings prevent us from doing that.

We must not lose sight for a moment that there are only two opposing forces that are continuously trying to control our thoughts. There is the Light and there is darkness. If we are not following the positive thoughts, we are undoubtedly following the negative thoughts. There is no such thing as a neutral force or in-between.

"For our struggle is not against flesh and blood, but against the rulers, against the authorities, against the powers of this dark world, and against the spiritual forces of evil in the heavenly realms." Ephesians 6:12 - NIV

Many people from various faiths earnestly believe that, by following the different rituals of their individual faith, they are earning the admission passes to the Kingdom of Heaven.

The strict following of various rituals can make one very religious person. But, to God, they are not important. They do not buy any special favors from Him, unless we change our hearts. What pleases Him is when we are personally sincere, honest, and true to Him. In order to be sincere and honest to Him we do not need to become strictly religious persons of any faith.

Many people also strongly believe that, if they can memorize their individual religious books or scriptures from the beginning to the end of their holy books, they will be closer to God. Let me emphasize from my own experience that when our time comes, when we will stand before Him, none of our religions, denominations, faiths, or the respective scriptures will accompany us.

We will stand there on our own, as an individual. I can assure you when each person will be standing there in front of Him each one of us will be viewed like His own child. This is the only identity we will have in front of Him. Nothing else will accompany us. He is not interested in which faith or to what denomination we belong. He wants to know what kind of a child I was when I lived on earth. Was I an obedient one to Him or a disobedient one to Him?

As I mentioned earlier, there are only two categories of our life here on earth. Did we follow after Christ? If we didn't, then we must have followed the evil one.

Following the evil one will consequently destroy us forever. For the people who are not religious but had their spiritual second births, there are only three attributes upon which He will judge us - how sincere, how true, and how honest we have been to Him in this life on earth. In other words, how pure was our heart? Everything else is secondary to Him.

He is not interested in whether we were black, brown, or white. He is not interested in whether we were citizens of a favored country. We already know that He is not interested in our religion, faith, or denomination. Let me reassure you that the only thing He is interested in from us as His own children is how genuine our personal relationships were with Him when we were living on earth.

The question may arise: what does He want from us? Does He want us to be happy? Does He want us to be joyful? Does He want us to be peaceful? The answer to all of them is "Yes." He wants us to be all of the above and beyond.

Then what is the primary thing that He is interested in from us? He is most interested in our genuine personal relationship. In order to build a genuine relationship, we must be true, honest, and sincere to Him.

To be sincere, true, and honest to Him, we'll definitely need to have the help from the Holy Spirit. Without Him, we will most certainly end up being unfaithful, insincere, and dishonest – exactly the opposite of what He wants from us.

He also knows that what He expects from us cannot be achieved without His divine help. He loved us so much that He Himself came down to earth in the form of a human being, lived among us, and showed us how to live our life here on earth. He also gave His human life as a sacrifice so that we can be spared from complete destruction. This is the Truth. He who had all the might and power to control the entire universe, why would He die in the hands of Evil ones? How is it possible?

The only answer to that is His unconditional love for us. He sacrificed His life for us so that we can change ourselves. As soon as we realize the Truth, we must surrender to His love and ask for His forgiveness.

He came down to earth on a mission to restore the full image that we had lost from the beginning by following the enemy. What does the full image and likeness of God look like? It looks like Christ! That's what I witnessed when I encountered Him. Christ is the exact likeness of God, the visible image of the invisible God, and the exact representation of His being.

God wants us, His children, to bear His image and likeness too. We were created to be like God, truly righteous and holy. In other words, we were created to be like Christ.

How many of us are like Him, even if we consider ourselves to be true followers of Him? Let's look at the inside of our hearts. What do we see? We see our heart is wicked and deceitful. If we find ourselves in that state, we should ask ourselves, who is in control of our heart?

A true follower of God is the person who is sincerely trying to be like Christ; one who follows after Him. Religion does not mean anything to Him. God is looking for a relationship. How is it possible?

He made it quite easy for us.

First, we must realize who we really are. We must also realize that this is not our real home. We are here for a short period of time. We must realize that we are all His children, and He wants us back to our real home. We also need to realize that we cannot free ourselves from our captivity without the Divine help.

Then we must accept the Truth that He came down to this world in human form in order to free us from our bondage. He sacrificed His human life and shed His blood for us. We must believe this Truth with all our hearts.

The very first step for us is to believe in Him - that He came down to rescue us from our captivity of darkness. Imagine the small child who has been lured away by the evil one with deception for his own pleasure. How would the little child ever free himself up from the captivity on his own unless a higher authority steps in? - Like police, parents, family members or friends.

Our situation is similar. We have been taken away from our real home with deception by the Evil One. Ever since, we are remaining as captives in this world of darkness, getting further and further away from our heavenly Father. Fortunately, our Father did not forsake us, did not abandon us. He loved us so much that He Himself came down upon this earth as a human and lived among us with no sin and yet sacrificed Himself so that we can live in our Father's home eternally forever. That's what He wants and that is His "key message" that I am sharing with each person regardless of their individual religion, culture, faith, or background. They are viewed as barriers in finding the Way to our real Home. Please read the following verses below - what the Apostle John is telling us about Jesus and the world. Jesus is the only Light in the world because He is God Himself in human form. Everything else in the world is darkness.

"For God so loved the world that he gave his one and only Son, that whoever believes in him shall not perish but have eternal life. 17 For God did not send his Son into the world to condemn the world, but to save the world through him. 18 Whoever believes in him is not condemned, but whoever does not believe stands condemned already because they have not believed in the name of God's one and only Son. 19 This is the verdict: Light has come into the world, but people loved darkness instead of light because their deeds were evil. 20 Everyone who does evil hates the light, and will not come into the light for fear that their deeds will be exposed. 21 But whoever lives by the truth comes into the light, so that it may be seen plainly that what they have done has been done in the sight of God." John 3:16-21 - NIV

Follow Jesus if you want to go through the Narrow Door

As Jesus was going through the towns and villages teaching, He made His way to Jerusalem.

23 Someone asked Him, "Lord, are only a few people going to be saved?" Jesus said to them, 24 "Make every effort to enter through the narrow door, because many, I tell you, will try to enter and will not be able to. 25 Once the owner of the house gets up and closes the door, you will stand outside knocking and pleading, 'Sir, open the door for us.'

"But He will answer, 'I don't know you or where you come from.' 26 "Then you will say, 'We ate and drank with you, and you taught in our streets.'

27 "But He will reply, 'I don't know you or where you come from. Away from me, all you evildoers!'" Luke 13:23-27, NIV

These powerful indications from the Lord are crystal clear. "Make every effort to enter through the Narrow Door." There is no other way.

This is the Narrow Door that I witnessed as I described earlier in my book. At that time, I was continuously looking at His Feet and pleading for His Mercy, when I noticed a very Narrow Door that was open for me to enter. All the other 12 Marvelous Gates that I witnessed were closed for me.

As I mentioned earlier, I looked slightly towards the left of the throne (right from my position) and was amazed to see a very narrow door. The door was so narrow that it struck me as completely out of proportion. I now realized that this narrow door is the only entrance-way to the inside of the Kingdom of Heaven and the only entrance in the entire perimeter of the compound that was open. This is the entrance for which I had been searching. Finally, I found it.

"How do I go through this door?" I asked myself. The Lord is so big and frightening that I cannot dare to go near the door. It was quite evident to me that I could not even try to enter through the door, unless the Lord allowed me to enter.

It had also been pretty clear to me that I was now standing at the Gateway to the Kingdom of Heaven, and I was completely at the mercy of the Lord.

I felt like running through the door. But I knew that would be an impossible task for me. The Lord is such a Giant sitting near the door, as if He is safeguarding the door. I could not dare to go through the door unless the Lord permitted me to do so. Nobody will dare to enter through that narrow door unless the Lord allowed him/her to do so.

Now I read in John Chapter 10 that Jesus has mentioned several times that He is the Gate (Entrance to the Narrow Door).

In John 10:9, **Jesus says,** *"I am the gate; whoever enters through me will be saved." - NIV*

Then in John 10:14-18 it is very clear what Jesus was referring to.

14 "I am the good shepherd; I know my sheep and my sheep know me – 15 Just as the Father knows me and I know the Father – and I lay down my life for the sheep. 16 I have other sheep that are not of this sheep pen. I must bring them also. They too will listen to my voice, and there shall be one flock and one shepherd. 17 The reason my Father loves me is that I lay down my life – only to take it up again. 18 No one takes it from me, but I lay it down of my own accord. I have authority to lay it down and authority to take it up again. This command I received from my Father." John 10:14-18, NIV

There is no doubt that Jesus is the Gate. He is the Narrow Door. In John 14:6, Jesus confirms, *"I am the way and the truth and the life. No one comes to the Father except through me.", NIV*

In the next verse, He is describing further who He really is. *"If you really know me, you will know my Father as well. From now on, you do know him and have seen him." John 14:7, NIV*

Wow! Who can dare to make a statement like this unless both the Father and Jesus are One?

From my experience, I'm absolutely certain that Jesus is the Narrow Door, and only through Him can I enter into the Kingdom of Heaven; only if He permits me to go through the Narrow Door next time when He sees me again. But how would I answer many people who asked me the questions: "Jesus cannot be the only Savior; what about all the other religious figureheads? Do all the roads not lead to Rome?"

Is Jesus the only Savior? My answer from my unexpected Encounter is absolutely 'yes'. My answer is firmed up when I read 1 Timothy 2:5. *"For there is one God and one mediator between God and mankind, the man Christ Jesus.", NIV*

What about all the religious figureheads? - Is there another person like Jesus anywhere in any religion? Please show me that person. There is none.

The birth of Jesus was divine. His life was sinless. His cruel death was pre-determined and divinely sacrificial to save all of us. His resurrection was unlike anything else throughout the history of mankind. It is only possible because of His Love for us. His Love was amazingly divine and unconditional, even though we do not deserve this. It shows how much He loves us. All other religious figureheads are simply men. They are all dead. None of them were resurrected. Only Jesus was, because He was God Himself.

Do all the roads not lead to Rome? No, all the roads do not lead to Rome. Jesus is the only Mediator between us and God, as we have seen in John 14:6 and 1 Timothy 2:5. From the beginning, God and mankind are at two opposite ends of a straight line. God is holy. We are just the opposite. We are sinful by nature. There is nothing to brag about that can make us holy. Jesus is God Himself, and He became man so that a perfect resolution can be provided to bring men and God together.

When we read the Bible and study the life of Jesus, His Message is clear - none of us can be saved on our own merits. It does not matter how religious we become or how hard we try to be good, we always fall short, because our heart is not pure, no matter what. That is why Jesus said to His Disciples, *"What is impossible with man is possible with God." Luke 18:27, NIV*

We can be saved only through Jesus, God's gift of Grace, His Mercy, and our faith.

8 "For it is by grace you have been saved, through faith – and this is not from yourselves, it is the gift of God – 9 Not by works, so that no one can boast. 10 For we are God's handiwork, created in Christ Jesus to do good works, which God prepared in advance for us to do." Ephesians 2:8-10, NIV

The question is: How do we qualify to go through the Narrow Door?

It is a four step process - Repent, Believe in Jesus Christ as the Son of God, Receive the Holy Spirit and Be Obedient to Him.

In each of these steps, what are most important are the sincerity, trueness, and honesty of our hearts.

The very first thing we must do is repent. Repent for what? Repent for our wrong doings or sins.

"For all have sinned and fall short of the glory of God." Romans 3:23, NIV

There is not a single person in the world who did not commit any sin. Therefore, everyone needs to repent. Genuine repentance is to feel sincere regret and dissatisfaction over some action or intention in the past, to change our mind about it, or to change our way. Repentance is coming to know that we were wrong, and we sinned against someone or against God.

Repent genuinely and turn to Jesus as our Savior.

"If you confess with your mouth that Jesus is Lord and believe in your heart that God raised him from the dead, you will be saved." Romans 10:9, NIV

Here again, the stress is on 'believe in your heart.' It refers to be a true belief, not a fake one, but a sincere one.

"To all who have received him, to those who believe in his name, he has given the right to become God's children." John 1:12, NIV

By turning from sin and seeking forgiveness in Christ and receiving Christ, we become the children of God. The entire process is sincere trust and faith in Christ. It is a total submission to Christ. And who is Christ? Christ is God Himself in human form known as the Son of God.

Surrendering to God Himself has nothing to do with any religion. Rather, it is a sincere heart-to-Heart transformation between a sinful person and his Creator, God Himself. Anyone from any religious background, whether we consider ourselves virtuous or sinners, wealthy or poor, healthy or ill, educated or uneducated, we can come directly to Jesus Christ who is God Himself in human form. He is saying, *"I will never turn away anyone who comes to me." John 6:37, NIV.*

The only requirement is our sincerity, our longing to trust in God, and to accept Christ, who is God's Son, as our Savior which must be genuine. The relationship between us and God Himself can be like a son/daughter to Father again. It is entirely a free gift to all of us, anyone who is willing to accept the gift. *"For it is by grace you have been saved, through faith – and this not from yourselves, it is the gift of God – not by works, so that no one can boast." Ephesians 2:8-9, NIV*

When we sincerely accept His gift, we are spiritually renewed and born again. And we are now sons and daughters of God, trusting in Jesus Christ, the One who paid the penalty for our sins when He died on the cross for us. We become new creations in God. *"Therefore, if anyone is in Christ, he is a new creation: the old is gone, the new has come!" 2 Corinthians 5:17, NIV*

Jesus never said to convert people from other religions and call them Christians of various denominations.

Jesus said, *19 "Therefore go and make disciples of all nations, baptizing them in the name of the Father and of the Son and of the Holy Spirit, 20 and teaching them to obey everything I have commanded you. And surely I am with you always, to the very end of the age." Matthew 28:19-20, NIV*

What did Jesus ask His Disciples to do? – Follow Me!

They were called the followers of Jesus until we see evidence in the Bible when Barnabas went to Tarsus to look for Saul, *26 "and when he found him, he brought him to Antioch. So for a whole year Barnabas and Saul met with the church and taught great numbers of people. The disciples were called Christians first at Antioch." Acts 11:26, NIV*

Since then, the followers of Jesus are called Christians, and rightfully so. But just by calling ourselves Christians does not change the basic principles of His discipleship. The basic principles are still the same.

It does not matter what we want to be called. The bottom line is that any of us who are "born again," accepts Christ as our Savior, and invites the Holy Spirit to enter into our life automatically becomes the disciple of Christ.

Our goal remains the same - to learn from our great Teacher, follow His teachings, and obey His instructions always. Our objective is to be like Him.

That does not mean we will be like Him immediately. It takes time to be disciplined to follow Him. We are humans. We are bound to make some mistakes along the way. Whenever we make a mistake and as soon as we realize it, we must immediately repent and ask for His forgiveness. We should also ask for the strength and the wisdom that we require so that we do not make the same mistake again. We must let the Holy Spirit guide us in transforming our lives. We must stay in sync with the Holy Spirit, no matter what. He promised that He would stay with us always, to the very end of age.

In order to start the discipleship process, Baptism is a necessary step. It is an act of submission, as well as an act of faith, on our part that results in a wonderful working of God in our lives. Our sins are washed away with the blood of Jesus. It is a spiritual rebirth through water and the Spirit.

However, Baptism is just the beginning. Then we must be taught. That means we need to be obedient students. We must be doers and not remain static. We also must grow to the point that we are obeying all the commandments that Jesus has taught us.

Nobody says that it is going to be an easy task to be a true follower of Jesus. We must not give up or deviate from reaching our goal of discipleship, which is to be like Him.

We also have an adversary that is real and quite powerful. He is going to try his best to derail us from achieving our goal. Just because we are baptized and decide to follow Christ does not stop the enemy from tempting us. I sincerely believe it is to the contrary. I also believe he is going to be out there with his full force to stop us from following Christ. He does not want us to worship God and to be the followers of Jesus. He wants us to fall in his traps so that we get further away from God. He wants us to worship him.

We can learn this from the events that took place after the Baptism of Jesus, when Jesus was led by the Spirit into the wilderness to be tempted by the devil. Three different times the devil came to Him and tempted Him to commit a mistake. On the third attempt, the devil took Jesus on a very high mountain and showed Him all the kingdoms of the world and their splendor. "All this I will give you," he said, "if you will bow down and worship me." Jesus said to him, "Away from me, Satan! For it is written: Worship the Lord your God, and serve him only." Then the devil left him, and the angels came and attended him.

Can we imagine how persistent and devious the devil is? If he can tempt Jesus, who is the Son of God, in that manner, what other schemes of things shall he have for you and me? And are we strong enough to resist the devil in the same manner as Jesus did?

Let us not underestimate the power of our enemy. He is the god of this world. He has blinded the minds of unbelievers so they cannot see the light of the gospel that displays the glory of Christ, who is the image of God. For the people that are genuinely "born again," it is very important that we remain in Christ always; otherwise, we may fall into the traps of our adversary. If we remain in Christ, we will have victory. The enemy cannot win over us unless we give him the foothold that he needs to come into our life and disrupt things. Should it happen in our life, there are three things that we must do in order to combat the disruption: Repent (a genuine one); Trust or Faith in Jesus (He only wants to see how sincere we are in our relationship with Him); and Pray for the Holy Spirit to intervene. Without the mighty power of the Holy Spirit, we might fall into his prey and become victims. The Bible tells us we can only fight back and win if we put on the Armor of God.

What is the Armor of God?

Every "born-again" follower of Christ must know how we can be equipped with the Armor of God. Threats against the "born-again" followers of Christ are real, and they can be serious. Apostle Paul has explained the steps in Ephesians 6:10-20 and I quote:

"10 Finally, be strong in the Lord and in his mighty power. 11 Put on the full armor of God, so that you can take your stand against the devil's schemes. 12 For our struggle is not against flesh and blood, but against the rulers, against the authorities, against the power of this dark world and against the spiritual forces of evil in the heavenly realms. 13 Therefore put on the full armor of God, so that when the day of evil comes, you may be able to stand your ground, and after you have done everything, to stand. 14 Stand firm then, with the belt of truth buckled around your waist, with the breastplate of righteousness in place. 15 and with your feet fitted with the readiness that comes from the gospel of peace. 16 In addition to all this, take up the shield of faith, with which you can extinguish all the flaming arrows of the evil one. 17 Take the helmet of salvation and the sword of the Spirit, which is the word of God. 18 And pray in the Spirit on all occasions with all kinds of prayers and requests. With this in mind, be alert and always keep on

praying for all the Lord's people. 19 Pray also for me, that whenever I speak, words may be given me so that I will fearlessly make known the mystery of the gospel, 20 for which I am an ambassador in chains. Pray that I may declare it fearlessly, as I should." Ephesians 6:10-20, NIV

It is important that we stand firm in our faith and let the Lord do battle for us. *"For the LORD your God is the one who goes with you to fight for you against your enemies to give you victory." Deuteronomy 20:4, NIV*

Jesus said that in this world His followers will have troubles, but in Him we will have peace.

"I have told you all these things, so that in me you may have peace. In this world you will have trouble. But take heart! I have overcome the world." John 16:33, NIV

Holy Spirit enters into our body and resides in us. The purpose of the Holy Spirit within us is to make us spiritually fit. He is going to mold us into the image of Christ, but we must act as obedient students always willing and cooperating to achieve that goal. With the Holy Spirit resident in our body, it becomes the holy temple, and we must treat it as such. We must flee from sin and not take up residence with sin and enjoy its pleasures.

No one is perfect, and it does not mean that the followers of Jesus will be perfect always. We will make a mistake here and there, from time to time. If it happens, we must pick ourselves up, genuinely repent for our sins, and ask for His forgiveness. Those who do the will of His Father will inherit the Kingdom of God. What is the will of His Father?

Repent genuinely and trust in Christ as your Savior.

"I tell you, no! But unless you repent, you too will perish." Luke 13:3, NIV

Let us pray for the unity in the body of Christ that each and every believer finds the Truth, obeys the Truth, and turns to be the follower of Truth. Let us not be hesitant in opening our hearts to Christ so that His Spirit can come and live within us and transform us to the true image of Christ. Christ dwells in our hearts through faith Ephesians 3:17. But we must be willing and obedient to Him for Him to make the changes happen within us. If we are unwilling and disobedient, then we are not listening to Him. That means we are not sincere and honest with Him. In that case, we are listening to ourselves or someone else. We cannot do the things of the flesh and still obey His commandments. Let us see what Apostle Paul is saying about us in Romans 8:5-11.

5 "Those who live according to the flesh have their minds set on the flesh desires; but those who live in accordance with the Spirit have their minds set on what the Spirit desires. 6 The mind governed by the flesh is death, but the mind governed by the Spirit is life and peace. 7 The mind governed by the flesh is hostile to God; it does not submit to God's law, nor can it do so." Romans 8:5-7, NIV

But, anyone who accepted the Christ as his/her Savior we are to live in accordance with the Spirit. Apostle Paul is urging us in Romans 8:5-7, NIV

12 "Therefore, brothers and sisters, we have an obligation – but it is not to the flesh, to live according to it. 13 For if you live according to the flesh, you will die; but if by the Spirit you put to death the misdeeds of the body, you will live." Romans 8:12-13, NIV

Apostle Paul is clearly saying that we have an obligation to live in accordance with the Spirit. We must make every attempt to live without sin. We must follow our great Teacher. It is not going to be an easy task, since we live in a world of captivity. But we must remain faithful, trusting Jesus, and let Him work through us. Generally speaking, sin originates in our heart and mind before it becomes a sinful act. As a follower of Christ, we should be able to end it right there. At the onset of any evil thought, we should surrender the thought to the Holy Spirit for Him to nail it on the cross, asking for His forgiveness, and to refill us with His Holy Spirit in our thoughts and minds. It works every time. But we must remain faithful to Him.

Sin has absolutely no room near our Holy God. That's the reason Jesus came down as a human to save us from the bondage of sin. Our salvation is not to be taken for granted. The precious 'Blood of Jesus' should never be considered as an Insurance that guarantees an auto entry into Heaven. It does not work that way. Neither does it mean that, since I'm saved, I go to my place of worship one day a week, and then I can do whatever I like for the other six days. I'm ok because I call myself a Christian.

If you are thinking that way my brothers and sisters, I urge you to study the Bible on a regular basis, on your own or with a group. You will find that we are all sinners saved by His Mercy or by His Grace alone, because He Himself came down to the earth and gave His life to save us. Why did He do that? Because He loves us so much that He cannot see us perish. The choice is up to each one of us: should we accept Him or reject Him? If we reject Him, there is no one who can save us. We are bound to have our eternal death. But, if we accept Him, we must accept the free gift of salvation in good faith and act accordingly.

When we accept the free gift of salvation, it implies a commitment to Him. What is that commitment? The commitment is a personal relationship between you and Him.

How fortunate are we, my brothers and sisters? The Creator of the entire universe is extending an open invitation to all mankind, regardless of our religion, race, culture, ethnicity or background. He says to all of us, "Come, accept me, I love you just the way you are, accept me. I'll give you the peace and joy that you need; you will never be hungry or thirsty; I give you eternal life because you are my precious child!"

And those of us who accepted His invitation are the lucky ones. With each one of us, He is eager to develop a personal relationship, one-on-One, a sincere one, a true one, and an honest one. Why does He want to do that? - Because He wants each one of us to be like Him.

Someone might think: Is He serious? He must be out of His mind. How can a sinful person like me ever be like Christ? It is impossible. He is God Himself in human form; He lived a sinless life when He lived among us; and here we are; buried in all kinds of sinful acts. We are dead people; how can we ever be like Him? It is absurd! We must go back to our own religions or to whatever lifestyles we are comfortable with. It is much easier for us to cope with that lifestyle.

Yes, it is impossible, and, to some extent, absurd for us because we are humans. We like to do our own thing, our own way, whatever pleases us. In Matthew 19:26, Jesus was saying to His disciples, ***"With man this is impossible, but with God all things are possible." – NIV***

It does not matter what we do or whatever we try, it is impossible for man to reach God. It does not matter how religious we are or how hard we try to score some points or favor with God. Everything is meaningless to Him, since we are sinful by nature, and He is holy. There is a wide gap between us. We can only come to God through His way, and His way is simple. We must repent for our sins and accept Christ as our Savior. After we do that, we must not stop right there. We need to continue listening to Him and working diligently with God so that His Holy Spirit can transform us to be like Christ.

To be a true Christian means to follow Christ truly. Accepting Christ in our individual life also means a full-time commitment to follow Him and to allow Him to take over every segment of our life, so that He can change us to become like Him. Otherwise, it is a journey with no rewards. Following Christ is also a commitment of genuine love and care between us and everyone else in our life. It is a commitment of love between us and our family members, between our spouses, between our children, between our neighbors, between us and others, above all between us and God.

Following Christ is also a big commitment for each one of us to obey His commandments. Someone asked Jesus, *"What must I do to inherit eternal life?" Jesus answered, "Love the Lord your God with all your heart and with all your soul and with all your strength and with all your mind; and Love your neighbor as yourself." Luke 10:27, NIV*

These are the two greatest commandments that Jesus asked all His followers to obey. In addition, we can find several commandments in the four gospels that Jesus expects us to obey. In John 14:15, Jesus says, *"If you love me, keep my commands" John 14:15, NIV*

Then, in John 14:23-24, Jesus is even more specific. *23 "Anyone who loves me will obey my teaching. My Father will love them, and we will come to them and make our home with them. 24 Anyone who does not love me will not obey my teaching. These words you hear are not my own; they belong to the Father who sent me." John 14:23-24, NIV*

Jesus is the One who saved me from my eternal death and gave me a second chance by sending me back to my family. He asked me to follow one guideline and five specific instructions when I'm still on earth. I mentioned them earlier in my book. Now, I want to obey all of His commandments because I love Him with all my heart. So what are His commandments for us? I started reading through the four gospels, and I found many of them. For the benefit of some of my Readers who may never read the Bible, I am quoting a few of His Commandments as examples for your review. This is not a complete list. Also, they are not in any specific order.

1. **Do not lose your integrity**. You are the salt of the earth. But if the salt loses its saltiness, how can it be made salty again? Matthew 5:13
2. **Let your light shine on the world**. You are the light of the world. A town built on a hill cannot be hidden. Matthew 5:14

3. **Place God First in your life**. But seek first his kingdom and his righteousness, and all these things will be given to you as well. Matthew 6:33

4. **End disputes quickly**. Settle matters quickly with your adversary who is taking you to court. Matthew 5:25

5. **Do not judge others**. For in the same way you judge others, you will be judged, and with the measure you use, it will be measured to you. Matthew 7:2

6. **Watch out for false prophets**. Watch out for false prophets. They come to you in sheep's clothing, but inwardly they are ferocious wolves. Matthew 7:15

7. **Humble yourself to serve others**. The greatest among you will be your servant. For those who exalt themselves will be exalted. Matthew 23:11-12

8. **Repent**. Repent, for the kingdom of heaven has come near. Matthew 4:17

9. **Store up your treasures in heaven**. Store up for yourselves treasures in heaven, where moths and vermin do not destroy, and where thieves do not break in and steal. For where your treasure is, there your heart will be also. Matthew 6:20-21

10. **Do not worry about the future**. Therefore do not worry about tomorrow, for tomorrow will worry about itself. Each day has enough trouble of its own. Matthew 6:34

11. **Love your enemies.** But I tell you, love your enemies and pray for those who persecute you. Matthew 5:44

12. **Abide in Me and I'll abide in you**. Remain in me, as I also remain in you. No branch can bear fruit by itself; it must remain in the vine. Neither can you bear fruit unless you remain in me. John 15:4

These are just a few examples of His commandments. There are many others. I encourage all my Readers to browse through the four gospels and finding them. Not only just finding them, but also to apply them in our day-to-day life. In this lost and broken world, The Bible is our only true Guide. It is similar to the modern day GPS that we use in our automobiles. Let us use it as often as possible when we are confused and uncertain about the direction we should take, let us not hesitate to meditate on the Scriptures and follow the guidance we receive from the Holy Spirit. Most importantly, let us remain in Christ until the end and He will remain with us until the end.

Take Care Of The Poor

"Take care of the poor. Open your hearts. Be generous to the poor. They need your help."

This was the final instruction from God to me.

Then, He repeated for the second time,

"TAKE CARE OF THE POOR. OPEN YOUR HEARTS. BE GENEROUS TO THEM. THEY NEED YOUR HELP. THIS IS VERY IMPORTANT."

(The word, "Poor," does not mean someone who needs financial help only; it can also mean someone who is physically, mentally, intellectually, emotionally or spiritually poor and needing help.)

When the Lord repeated for the second time asking me to take care of the poor and stressing that I must be generous to the poor as they need my help, I realized this is a very important instruction.

I said very humbly to the Lord, "Lord! Certainly I will help the poor as much as I can. You know the needs of the poor in the world are far greater than what a small person like me can do. The needs are not only where I live; the needs are everywhere, all over the world."

"Lord! Please forgive me for saying this. I will take care of the poor as much as I can, but my efforts will be like a tiny drop of water in the entire ocean. It is not going to make much of an impact."

As I said this to God, I was feeling extremely concerned that I should not have said anything like this to God. Definitely, He will be angry at me, and He will be very annoyed with me. I have no right to speak to Him like this. Who am I to tell God? He knows how big the needs are.

It is with great fear and great respect I said to the Lord, "Lord! Please forgive my sins. I should not have said anything like this to You. You are Almighty. You know everything. I did not mean to question your instruction. I am a simple human being. I am only trying to state that the needs to help the poor are far greater than what a small person like me can accomplish. Please forgive me. I beg for Your mercy!"

I was waiting for God to get angry at me and punish me for my rudeness. However, I was pleasantly surprised, as I noticed that He was not annoyed with me at all. Instead, with a deep loving voice, He said to me, "Listen carefully! I am assigning you with a few tasks when you are back on the earth. I want you to complete your unfinished tasks. When you are back to the earth I want you to write two books."

He continued, "Go back and write the first book about telling the Truth; about your experience; and about this conversation as it is taking place between you and Me. Do not be afraid to be truthful. I will ensure that this book reaches to the readers everywhere in the world."

The Lord looked at me and said, "For these tasks I am also giving you two guidelines for you to follow. You must remember them always. They are important."

"First, each and every penny that you will receive from the sales of the two books you must give them away to the cause of the poor. You must not keep one penny from the proceeds for yourself. This is very important!"

"Second, you must let your readers know that it is not important to Me at all what church, temple, or religious institution they belong. The most important thing to Me is each person's own personal relationship with Me. I am only interested to know how sincere, how honest, how true they are with Me."

"Tell your readers that the five instructions that I am asking you to obey between now and your next time, the same instructions equally apply to all mankind. The fifth instruction is particularly important to each and every person. Everyone needs to open their hearts and be generous to the poor. I expect it from everyone."

That's where our conversation at the Gateway to the Kingdom of Heaven ended. I returned to my second life only through His Mercy and through His Grace. I complied with all His Instructions. This is how I was born again. Today, I'm a new person. He has used the two books for me as my bases to know Him intimately who He is and also for me to grow in Him. It will be appropriate for me to say that He asked me to write the two books primarily for myself. Now, I'm combining the two books with my personal interpretation and understanding for the benefit of anyone who wants to know the Truth and ***accept my Savior as yours***. If you find Him knocking on your door (heart) listen to what He is saying to you,

28 "Come to me, all you who are weary and burdened, and I will give you rest. 29 Take my yoke upon you and learn from me, for I am gentle and humble in heart, and you will find rest for your souls. 30 For my yoke is easy and my burden is light." Matthew 11:28-30 - NIV

Bible Credits